"Sean systematically shows you how to break down some of the biggest wealth creation strategies—a must read for anyone looking to create real wealth."

    - Kc Chohan, Founder of Together CFO

"Sean is on a mission to help people save more of their hard earned money, while also showing them how they can strategically give it away more effectively."

    - Caleb Guilliams, Founder of BetterWealth

"I've never met a more selfless, genuine, and helpful person in my life. You won't either. Never once has Sean said what he wants, but always from the perspective of 'How can I help you achieve your goals?' Whenever I applied resistance, his inner Socrates came out, and he directed his questions right at my own obstacle that I put up."

    - Preston, business student with a focus in real estate investing

"Because of working with Sean, I now have improved confidence that I can 'weather the financial storms' that may arise in the next 10-20 years by being smart about money and investing now, using Sean's connections and alternative strategies. Sean is here to help and can be trusted because, after working with him over the years, he has proven those qualities time and again."

    - Vishal, major airline pilot

The Truth About Taxes:

How the Wealthy Elite Play a Different Game

Sean Briscombe

Published by Author Academy Elite
PO Box 43, Powell, OH 43065
www.AuthorAcademyElite.com

Identifiers:

LCCN: 2021907564
ISBN: 978-1-64746-768-5 (paperback)
ISBN: 978-1-64746-769-2 (hardback)
ISBN: 978-1-64746-770-8 (ebook)

Available in paperback, hardback, e-book, and audiobook

All Scripture quotations, unless otherwise indicated, are taken from the Holy
Bible, New International Version®, NIV®. Copyright © 1973, 1978, 1984 by
Biblica, Inc.™ Used by permission of Zondervan. All rights reserved worldwide.

Any Internet addresses (websites, blogs, etc.) and telephone numbers printed
in this book are offered as a resource. They are not intended in any way to be
or imply an endorsement by Author Academy Elite, nor does Author Academy
Elite vouch for the content of these sites and numbers for the life of this book.

Some names and identifying details have been changed
to protect the privacy of individuals.

TABLE OF CONTENTS

PREFACE

You may be wondering how this book came to be and how I came to write it. After all, I am not a tax planner, do not have a tax preparation license, nor am I an expert in tax code.

I actually stumbled upon the 1041 trust and foundation system by accident, and I have a team of experts for legal and tax counsel to help me with the process I am going to outline in this book. These experts are at the top of their fields in constitutional law, contract law, and tax law. I can say with confidence that the team that files my tax returns is the best in the country. They hold the highest nationally regulated licenses available to anyone in the field.

The Truth About Taxes is about my experience with the 1041 system, and my own journey of discovery, growth, and contribution. I encour-age you to read the tax code in order to learn how it might apply to you and your business. Don't rely on another person to make your decisions for you. Nothing in this book should be taken as advice or counsel. You have to hire your own team or engage with experts who know this stuff inside and out. Sean Briscombe, LLC and its affiliates do not provide tax, legal, or accounting advice. The material contained herein has been prepared for informational purposes only, and is not intended to provide, and should not be relied on for, tax, legal or accounting advice. You should consult your own tax, legal, and accounting advisors before engaging in any transaction.

You should not act or refrain from acting on the basis of any legal information contained herein without first seeking legal advice from counsel in the relevant jurisdiction. Only your individual tax, legal, and accounting advisors can provide assur-ances that the information contained herein—and your interpretation of it—is applicable or appropriate to your particular situation. This material may contain links to third-party websites. Such links are only for the convenience of the reader and Sean Briscombe LLC does not endorse the contents of the third-party sites.

"I believe people have to follow their dreams—I did."
- Larry Ellison, former Oracle CEO

CHAPTER ONE
MY JOURNEY OF DISCOVERY

In 2008, I was newly married, passionate, and ready to conquer the world. My wife and I had one desire: to start our family. Naturally, we were ecstatic when we found out my wife was pregnant. We picked out the name Charlie before we knew if we were having a boy or a girl, but I secretly hoped we'd have a girl. Our excitement built as we set up the nursery for her arrival. We could not wait to start this new chapter of our lives. Everything in our young marriage was going as planned.

Ever since I was a boy, I lived my life according to plans I made in order to check off the next box and accomplish my next lofty goal. I grew up the son of two middle-class parents, who worked hard from 9 a.m. to 5 p.m. I trained at a high level as a diver my whole life, and I eventually earned a scholarship to dive for Southern Methodist University. My aspirations were to be on a Wheaties box and win an Olympic gold medal. In college, I started out as a biology major, but diving took priority over studying. If you had told me I would eventually get into business, finance, or anything related to my current profession, I would have thought you were crazy. I had no interest in anything related to that line of work. Biology didn't really interest me either, though. Since I focused on fitness so much and enjoyed training others, I ended up majoring in physical therapy, and I got a job with a practice right out of college. In exchange for 10-hour days, I earned a salary, received health benefits, and started contributing to a 401(k).

That is what middle-class Americans are expected to do, after all. That is what I was taught safety and security looked like. You work hard in school, land a good job, earn a salary, and contribute to a pension, all to retire with a gold watch and a 401(k). I was educated to be a great employee, not to think like a business owner, which is how the wealthy elite educate their children. They pass down knowledge of marketing, accounting, investments, tax code, and much more from generation to generation, as you will soon find out in great detail.

By the time I got married in 2008, my career had taken several turns, and I had my own real estate and mortgage company. However, the economic collapse from the subprime mortgage meltdown soon forced me to shut it down, and my losses were accumulating. I had been in real estate lending and investing for six years at that point, and I was becoming more uncertain and fearful about the industry. How could anyone win the game of investing if this was our new normal?

The bottom fell out from under me later that year when we lost our daughter, Charlie, due to a miscarriage. I was telling myself the story of self-pity, that I'd never become a dad or create a legacy. Everything my wife and I had hoped for when we got married earlier in the year seemed like a distant dream. Our plan went off the rails, and we fell from cloud nine into a pit of despair.

For years, my wife had been told she could never have children. When she was 20, she had been diagnosed with interstitial cystitis and endometriosis. Her doctors wanted to remove her uterus, which she did not allow. When we first met, she told me she didn't believe she could have children, yet she held onto hope that one day she would have a baby. Knowing how far-fetched her chances of getting pregnant were made the miscarriage even more devastating. Little did we know that it wasn't about our plan, it was about God's plan.

As you can imagine, I was desperate and in bad shape mentally and emotionally, but we weren't ready to give up on our dream of starting a family. Through our church, we became friends with a couple who had started going through the process to get their foster care license. They approached us to see if we wanted to go through the classes with them. We were reluctant, as our wounds were still fresh from our loss, but we decided to explore the option. As we moved on with our lives and became friends with this couple, we began to imagine ourselves with a family again.

While we were taking classes to become foster parents, we also decided to try in vitro fertilization. We made several attempts to get pregnant, but we weren't successful at that time. Despite these setbacks, we were still hesitant to become foster parents. We were just so afraid of the unknown. Ultimately, though, we decided to finish the licensing process.

We were also persuaded to become foster parents when we learned some devastating statistics about the children who needed our help. According to the most recent numbers available from Pathways Youth and Family Services, in 2018, there were 17,500 Texas children in foster care. The state also had 280,911 reported allegations of child abuse or neglect. I guarantee the COVID-19 pandemic has made those numbers dramatically increase. Buckner International Foster Care and Adoption, an agency based in Dallas, reports that 62% of children in the foster care system were removed from their homes due to neglect, and 36% due to parent drug abuse. Thirty-five percent of the children in Texas foster homes have been bounced around to more than two placements, according to the Kids Count Data Center. Some of the youngest children need help the most, as 48% of children in the Texas foster care system are five and under.

The children in my state need loving homes more than ever, so my wife and I stepped up to help. In our experience, Texas Health and Human Services needed foster parents right away. Almost immediately after getting our license we received a phone call about fostering two sisters, ages 2 and 5. They had been rescued from a one-room apartment where they lived with their parents and four other siblings. When their parents were busted for cooking meth (which is a huge problem in Texas), Child Protective Services took all six children to a group home. The home did not have enough beds for the two youngest sisters, so we ended up getting the call. My wife and I took care of them for three months before they went to live with their aunt in Dallas. We still keep in touch.

After they left, we were contacted about fostering a three-year-old girl, who we were later blessed to be able to adopt. The police found her hiding in the bathtub of a hotel room surrounded by food wrappers and half-eaten jars of peanut butter marked with her finger prints from scooping it out like a spoon. A SWAT team had swarmed the hotel after suspecting meth activity, and they stumbled upon the largest check fraud scheme in Texas history, run by the little girl's birth mother and grandfather. She was hiding under a blanket, and the police said it looked like she used the bathtub as her bed and occasionally had food thrown in to her by an adult. All of her teeth had been capped with silver, as many children in similar situations are fed juice in bottles from infancy, instead of milk or formula. There was also a scar on her back from some sort of sharp object.

Child Protective Services placed her in short-term care for a few days until they alerted us that there was a child in need of a permanent place to live. We gave her the first real place she could call home. Her mother had been in and out of jail, and the poor girl had been bounced around between friends' homes. After fostering her for a year, we went through the adoption process and gave her a forever home. Our daughter, like many children in the foster system, was originally diagnosed with Oppositional Defiant Disorder and Reactive Attachment Disorder, a condition in which an infant or child doesn't establish healthy attachments with parents or caregivers, according to the Mayo Clinic. It develops when a child's basic needs for comfort, affection, and nurturing aren't met. We didn't learn that this was a misdiagnosis for 10 years, after more comprehensive psychological analysis was done. A new, and more accurate, diagnosis of Disruptive Mood Dysregulation Disorder, immediately made us reexamine our parenting strategies. Due to the misdiagnosis, we thought that her mood swings and defiance stemmed from anxiety and control issues. However, it turns out that she is so afraid of her own emotions that she doesn't want to talk about them, or even feel them, which is why her brain disrupts them.

She desires to please us more than anything. For example, if we told her to clean her room, she would go upstairs and stuff everything under her bed. After all, we didn't tell her how to clean it, and it was, technically, clean. For 10 years, my wife and I attributed this to being oppositional. We thought she was trying to control the situation and "stick it to us," since she didn't want to do what we asked. We would find everything piled underneath her bed and get confused, then we'd become angry with her when she was just trying to please us. There is no way to tell how common this type of misdiagnosis is in foster children, since these are all common disorders that result from experiencing childhood trauma, but it shows how important mental health care is for these children.

We soon received a call about caring for another pair of sisters, a two-year old and a nine-month old. The sisters had been abandoned by their birth mother with the infant strapped into a high chair. When the police entered their tiny apartment, they found the two-year-old trying to feed her sister Cheerios. After they stayed with us for a year, we considered finding another family for them. The foster system deemed our home "full" with three children, and we desired to help more children. Eventually, we found another family that we were all comfortable with, but we still see them all the time. In fact, we are their Godparents, and our daughters consider them sisters.

Later, we fostered and adopted another infant. She came to us after her birth father shot her mother in front of her when she was five months old. When the police arrived, her father put her under blankets and clothes to attempt to hide her in the closet. Her parents were also involved with meth, which led to abuse and neglect. When children don't have basic needs, such as nutrition, love, attention, and touch, met it affects their brain chemistry and how they interact with the world. Now, she is a well-adjusted child. Later, my wife became pregnant and gave birth to our third daughter to complete our family.

As soon as we started fostering, we knew that was what we were meant to do, and it became our mission. I began to research how to set up a 501(c) (3) for the purpose of helping more children. I wanted to start an organization that would provide resources, training, and support to kids in foster care and the adults who cared for them.

I was still struggling to grow my real estate lending and investing business, and it seemed impossible to provide for my family and set aside enough money to help more foster families in the way I desired. My challenge was that the more money I made, the more I owed in taxes. Due to the additional tax deductions at the business level, I had to spend more of what I earned just to lower my tax burden. This didn't help me keep my money, grow my money, or give back to foster children. I didn't see how I could be of much help to the kids who needed it.

Hunting an elusive strategy

Throughout my career in finance, I have been hunting for better strategies for my clients and myself. I was searching for something, but I had no idea what it looked like until I stumbled on it by accident.

In 2010, I was working with an entrepreneur who would soon become a legend in the internet marketing game. A few years earlier, he made a small fortune doing marketing work for companies, and he started talking to finance professionals about how to invest. The big financial companies all told him to invest in mortgage-backed securities (MBS). At the same time, he was committed to making wise choices with his new-found financial gains and was skeptical about what he was seeing. He couldn't put his finger on it, but he knew something was wrong with the real estate market, so he kept his money in cash. When Lehman Brothers crashed, he knew he had dodged a bullet.

In response to the housing-market crash, he created a financial education platform to teach people the black box secrets that the wealthy use to manage their money. He brought me in as one of his first advisors. He also hired Tom Wheelwright, a leading expert in wealth and tax strategy, as a CPA. Wheelwright had worked with some business heavyweights, including Robert Kiyosaki, founder of Rich Global LLC and author of *Rich Dad, Poor Dad: What the Rich Teach Their Kids about Money That the Poor and Middle Class Do Not*. Wheelwright has written several tax strategy books, and is still viewed as the go-to guy for tax strategy in the internet marketing game. He was able to bring a ton of tax strategy content to the platform to show members. Needless to say, the group was a financial dream team. The thing that kept bugging me, though, was that all of the strategies these guys promoted operated in the 1040 tax system and revolved around LLCs, S corps, and C corps. In my opinion, these were not black box secrets, they were just regular tax strategies.

Everyone involved in that platform made a bunch of money, but I was left still searching for elusive and revolutionary strategies. My journey brought me to a CPA from Missouri who had some unique methods. He was the CFO for a clean coal production company that had the technology to extract nitrogen and sulfur from piles of laid up coal, which could then be used as fertilizer. Each ton of clean coal produced a certain amount in tax credit. The company raised capital by transferring credits to investors at 50 cents on the dollar. It was a unique way of lowering taxes by investing in clean energy. I ended up hiring him as the internal controller for both of my businesses and to handle my personal finances. This turned out to be a huge mistake; a few years later I found out that he was running a Ponzi scheme.

My wife and I were in panic mode because our finances were in such disarray, but the worst part was learning that the mess we were in was not uncommon. A lot of people find themselves in similar situations because they put blind trust in their CPA and aren't actually watching what's going on. When you sign your tax return, you take responsibility for everything in it. If the IRS knocks on your door, you have to decide whether you're going to fight the audit process or help the IRS do its job. Trust me, based on my experience, all IRS agents want to do is close a file and move to another one in their huge stack. We weren't trying to hide anything from the government. We just hired a guy who didn't do his job, and we made the mistake of trusting him. Let me rephrase that: he lied about doing his job and created fake evidence so we wouldn't become suspicious.

I continued to do a lot of research while we were cleaning up our financial mess. While I was working with the IRS, I stumbled upon information about trusts and foundations. After looking into what types of trusts were out there, and discovering that there were more than 86 unique types or structures, I began interviewing CPAs, attorneys, and other experts searching for the best structure to accomplish my goals. I was shown a type of structure that not a lot of tax experts know about. In fact, this information is typically reserved for tax professionals known as Enrolled Agents. This is the highest accolade the IRS gives to tax professions. Enrolled Agents are federally licensed and can prepare taxes in any U.S. state or territory. The vast majority of tax professionals are only licensed to work in a single state, something we will go into much more detail about later. My mission became tracking down an Enrolled Agent. Through a long line of networking, and introductions from extremely wealthy people, I finally found one.

My quest for a brilliant strategy ended when I met with an Enrolled Agent, and a personal journey of transformation began. This wasn't some new trick to add to my 1040 tax return, it was a whole new system: the 1041 system. A 1041 tax return with a specialized private trust can help you keep the money you earn and grow it in a system of trusts and foundations.

I wanted to jump in right away to save my money from Uncle Sam, grow that wealth, and use it to benefit and to bless the foster community instead. I also felt that I needed to teach others to do the same thing so they could support causes they were passionate about. I was pumped to get started, but first I had to fix my own tax mess. I had to clean up several calendar years of taxes. Before I could teach it to anyone else, I needed to clean my own house and successfully implement the system myself.

I also had to convince my wife that moving to the 1041 system was the best move for us. It sounds like a no brainer, right? The end game is saving the money you would have paid the government, growing it with uninterrupted compounding interest, and funding a cause you're passionate about. But there's a catch. Another discovery I made about the system is that you must give up ownership (without giving up control) of all of your assets. This is the part a lot of my clients get stuck on, and was a point of contention with my wife, as well. We had just gone through a nightmare financial situation, were lucky to make it out with any assets left, and all of a sudden I was pushing to give up ownership of our house, cars, incomes, and everything else. She came around after some tough conversations and became more open to the idea after learning that if we gave up ownership of all our stuff, we could no longer be hunted by the IRS.

The next hurdle we'd need to clear was explaining what we were doing to our family and friends. Most of them thought that we were crazy. A lot of them still can't make sense of it years later after seeing our success in the 1041 system. They can't fathom how we went from such a low period in our lives, with the loss of our baby and the audit, to the pendulum swinging the opposite way, collapsing time, and now living in abundance with our focus on philanthropy.

Funding our passion

You'll soon discover that a major theme in this book is discovering your purpose. I'll present potential strategies you can use to set up your finances, but you will only be successful in this journey if you have a desire to fund those passions. We stumbled into becoming foster parents due to tragic circumstances, and we were hesitant if it was the right decision for us, at first. Now, I can't imagine life any other way. Thanks to the 1041 system, we've been able to, and will continue to, bless countless foster families. There are approximately 20,000 children bouncing around the foster care system in Texas. Our family foundation has magnified the impact we've been able to make.

My wife and I started The Kind Foundation in 2017 to do exactly what our mission and purpose statement says: To "Help kids heal from life's hurts." A huge part of what we do deals with the mental health of children in foster care. We are dedicated to preventing misdiagnosis, like our daughter experienced, and getting these children the best level of mental health care. Our foundation provides donations, gifts, and grants for all types of training and neuroscience research, which allows foster children to rewire their brains. The development and understanding of how trauma affects the brain, and brain chemistry, is changing the way therapists are approaching the issues of trauma and neglect and helping those children heal. Children in foster homes often grow up believing that nobody loves them, thinking 'even my mother must not have loved me enough to keep me around,' convinced that they have nothing to contribute, and feeling that nobody wants them in their forever family. We contribute to agencies that help kids shift and rewire neuropathways so these negative stories can be interrupted so that they can reflect on what is true and what is possible for them in their lives. Instead of saying "nobody loves me" while they are in foster care, they can shift their mindset and reprogram their brain to have confidence, clarity, and certainty. They learn to tell themselves "I'm valuable. I'm worthy. I'll wait here while my forever family prepares my home for me."

Some of our donations help fund doctors' research on healing traumatic brain injuries, such as PTSD or childhood trauma. The Kind Foundation also donates the neuroscience kits doctors have developed as part of that research, which can improve gut health, brain health, emotional health, and focus for children who have suffered trauma. We also contribute to a child development institute, which helps children who suffer from the effects of early trauma, neglect, or abuse. One of the most fascinating things we do is help foster children get access to Eye Movement Desensitization and Reprocessing (EMDR) therapy. These techniques are similar to how doctors treat soldiers for PTSD and literally help kids shift and rewire neuropathways by developing new patterns and habits in their brains.

None of this would be possible if I hadn't learned how to legally and ethically stop the bleeding caused by paying sickening amounts in taxes every year. Thanks to learning and implementing this private trust structure, I can keep my tax dollars just like politicians, professional athletes, and other members of the wealthy elite. Additionally, I can grow and protect my business and my family's wealth for generations by keeping those assets in a trust and safe from taxes, lawsuits, interest expenses, and inflation. The rest of this book will lead you on a journey of creating a financial legacy that will outlive you, your kids, and even their kids into perpetuity inside a private family foundation, just like more than 200,000 wealthy families already do in the United States. This is literally the No. 1 wealth-building strategy on the planet.

"The raising of extraordinarily large sums of money, given voluntarily and freely by millions of our fellow Americans, is a unique American Tradition… Philanthropy, charity, giving voluntarily and freely… call it what you like, but it is truly a jewel of an American tradition."

- President John F. Kennedy

CHAPTER TWO
SHIFTING YOUR MINDSET

Most people are taught from a young age that in order to build our wealth we must own more assets. That is why we go out looking to spend our money and invest our wealth as soon as we have any. We accumulate things such as homes, cars, boats, more properties, more land, etc. If you do that (and most people do), then you must file a 1040 tax return and pay taxes according to what you own. Those are the rules of the 1040 game. Taxes follow title. That's a phrase you'll see a lot in this book because it's the backbone of the system that most Americans know and follow.

If you give up ownership of your assets without giving up control, then you are taxed according to trust accounting. Yes, clients love to hear that they'll be losing less money to the tax man. However, a lot of them decide not to move forward in the process because they can't think through how giving up their stuff works for them. They get stuck and confused, and a confused mind always says "no." I lose some clients here, but that's fine. It's best that we split ways, because what I'm looking for are giving leaders who have a cause they are passionate about funding. If they get hung up on ownership, and can't comprehend how the 1041 structure will allow them to give back in a more impactful way, then they don't have the right mindset and they aren't a good fit anyway.

I had a potential client recently who wanted to sell his business for more than $90 million. When we got to talking, I discovered that he only cared about saving tax dollars, not the private foundation, or the "legacy and philanthropy" conversation. I knew he would have a hard time shifting his mindset to become a giving leader. This type of businessman will likely end up doing something outside the rules of the 1041 system. They may create a situation where they use trust money to benefit themselves with personal-use items, such as food, fuel, entertainment, or fashion. If you don't want to help benefit other people, then you don't have a mindset that will allow you to give up ownership without giving up control.

Clients I have successfully led through this mindset shift feel an immediate relief along with a sense of purpose. When you give up ownership of your stuff, it shifts who you are and what you do on a daily basis. When you finally commit, your focus shifts from accumulation and growth to contribution.

A case study in philanthropy

Both of my parents worked at Stanford University when I was growing up. My mom was a medical technologist who worked at the university's hospital, and my dad worked as an engineer supervising the power facilities on campus. They both earned a salary and rarely received bonuses. They faithfully saved their income, stashed some in retirement accounts, and quickly paid off debts.

My mom's mindset on income baffled me. During high school, I remember telling her about my friend's dad, John Arrillaga, who is a real estate entrepreneur in Silicon Valley. I had spent time on their family "farm," as they liked to call their ranch in the foothills of Northern California. It was in the heart of the extremely affluent town of Woodside, California. I used to go there during the summer to help my friend, John Arrillaga Jr., plant trees. They also had a full staff who managed the ranch, but John's dad taught his children the value of hard work. We were mainly out there based on principle, but as payment for the hard work, we got to enjoy four- wheeling and partying on the property. In retrospect, however, John Sr. was teaching John Jr. (as well as his friends) how to be the best Trustee of their family trust for the benefit of future beneficiaries. Planting trees is the ultimate illustration of "being a good trustee" in the 1041 system. As John's dad used to quip with us, "When is the best time to plant a tree, boys?" To which he'd continue, "30 years ago! When is the second best time to plant a tree?" And then he'd drop the lesson—"today!"

Arrillaga Sr. is an icon in Palo Alto today, and his family's name is adorned on the side of many prominent buildings on the Stanford campus. He actually worked closely with my dad to complete his visions for aesthetically pleasing student housing and campus facilities. My dad was responsible for coordinating the power and utilities for all buildings on campus, and they grew to be good friends and colleagues.

One day, I was browsing a magazine and stumbled upon Mr. Arrillaga's net worth. When I mentioned the value to my mom, she responded by saying "Ugh, what a pain."

'That's it,' I thought to myself. 'My mom has gone insane.'

When I asked her why she would say that, she explained, "I would never want to be that rich. Can you imagine all the taxes he has to pay?"

My 17-year-old brain couldn't compute her logic. Who in his or her right mind wouldn't want to be a billionaire? Who wouldn't want to have so much money that they could literally help hundreds of people with gifts, grants, donations, training, and other resources? That was my parents' mindset, though.

My mom didn't comprehend that Arrillaga Sr. doesn't pay taxes the way she is used to paying them. She couldn't understand a world she didn't know. Through business trusts, family trusts, and private foundations, Mr. Arrillaga has literally saved billions of dollars in taxes over the decades and redirected that capital into philanthropic endeavors. That is only possible because he does not personally own any of his income or assets. Money comes into his business, bills are paid, and the rest is distributed into his trusts. In those trusts, bills are also paid, assets are bought and sold, increasing or decreasing the "corpus" of the trust (something we go into with clients), and the rest is distributed, or donated, to charity through his private foundations. Since his income doesn't come to him, he's not personally responsible for taxes, which fall to the trusts and businesses. Now, imagine what you could do with that extra money if you could save it and grow it all through the years. I'm talking taxes at every level: city, county, state, and federal.

If you want to see a real-life example of "venture philanthropy," just look at what the Arrillaga family has accomplished. That family is living a life of meaning and purpose. The world opened up to them when they started asking how they could make a bigger impact. I remember walking around the Stanford campus with Mr. Arrillaga when I was a high school senior training with the college diving team (something that the NCAA allowed back then). We discussed how the campus had become a second home to me since I began training there when I was eight. He asked me about my diving schedule, how often I traveled, and how I managed to keep up in school while being so busy. While we walked, we passed a piece of trash on the ground. He stopped, picked it up, and handed it to me. I must have given him a funny look, and he responded by saying "never walk by trash without picking it up. Always leave a place looking better than it did when you got there." This guy had given millions of dollars to Stanford, yet here he was picking trash up off the ground. This is something I'll always remember. To this day, when I'm around town with my daughters, we pick up trash and I tell them the same thing.

I will also always remember meeting my childhood hero at the Arrillaga house. Later on, during my senior year of high school, John Arrillaga Jr. called me up one night to go have dinner at Pedro's, a popular Mexican restaurant his family owned near the Stanford campus. When I arrived at his house before dinner, I walked in to see Bill Walsh, then Head Coach of the San Francisco 49ers at the time. Walsh is now a Hall of Famer, but this was back in the '80s, when he and Joe Montana were leading the 49ers to Super Bowl Championships. I grew up idolizing the man.

Walsh and his wife were heading out to dinner with Mr. Arrillaga and his wife. I'm sure they were in a rush to get to dinner, however, Mr. Arrillaga still took the time to introduce me to Mr. and Mrs. Walsh. He talked me up as much as he could and told him I was training with the U.S. Diving Team. I left there in shock and ate my dinner in silence that night. I just couldn't believe someone as important as Mr. Arrillaga would talk so highly of me to someone as famous as Bill Walsh. That's just the type of guy he is, though.

He has dedicated his life to making the world better and more beautiful for others. Laura Arrillaga-Andreessen, his daughter, teaches a course at Stanford about giving and philanthropy. Her book *Giving*

2.0: Transform Your Giving and Our World explains what is possible from a philanthropic standpoint if you create a system of identifying, analyzing, and supporting charities. What I find most interesting, though, is what her course and book leave out. She does a great job teaching philanthropic strategies and assessing the places people support financially.

However, she doesn't say anything about her foundation or the Arrillaga Foundation, which is one of a few her father started. She also doesn't mention that her father's foundation files a 990- PF and is a private foundation with more than $27 million growing tax free.

Laura's late mother, Frances, was a tireless fundraiser who worked closely with the Stanford Office of Development as a member of the Major Gifts Committee. Her influence remains present on campus through her past nomination of alumni to the university's Board of Trustees. Stanford named the Frances C. Arrillaga Alumni Center in honor of her "courage, boundless enthusiasm, and unfailing devotion to her alma mater, her community, and her family."

Frances Arrillaga was a leader in her community, serving on boards of several Bay Area organizations, including Menlo School (where John Jr. and I attended high school), Castilleja School (where her daughter Laura went), the Palo Alto Medical Foundation, the Peninsula Center for the Blind and Visually Impaired, the YMCA, the Peninsula Bridge program, Family Services of the Mid-Peninsula, Silicon Valley Community Foundation, and Avenidas (senior services for Mid-Peninsula). Laura is still doing amazing work furthering that legacy, and has impacted thousands of lives for the better. That legacy will continue for generations due to the family's commitment, hard work, and knowledge of the tax code.

Taxes follow title

There's another part to the phrase "taxes follow title" that I need to explain. Whoever owns the income or assets is taxed according to the tax code, which was written and approved by the legislature. Congress writes the tax code for all Americans who file a 1040 tax return. If your income is based on W-2 wages, the 1099 form, or if you set up an S Corp, a C Corp, or a traditional LLC, ultimately every dollar of your income and production falls on the 1040 tax return.

You're already familiar with the global economy, the national economy, and even the local economy. However, you also have a personal economy that is no different. You must understand your personal economy in order to protect yourself, your family, and your legacy from the five major outside influences that erode your wealth: taxes, interest expense, inflation, lawsuits, and judgments (such as in divorce).

As money comes into your personal economy, your team of tax professionals goes to work doing what they've been taught to do through their state-licensed training. They probably have decent strategies to minimize taxes by using LLC, S Corp, and C Corp structures to leverage the tax code. They're good at what they've been trained to do, and you've probably paid them a lot of money. It's not their fault that their focus remains on 1040 tax returns. Remember, 99% of their clients are in that world, and that's where their core business income and revenue comes from. They understand ownership, taxation, and how that affects what you can and cannot do. That's why if you were to ask them if income is taxable at different rates, and about the rules of the game based on who owns it, they should be able to confirm that.

How you hold your assets determines how you will be taxed on them. If you want to hold onto them personally, you'll follow the rules of the game for the 1040 tax return, and you'll be taxed at the current rates based on that code. This is one of the main reasons people put assets into an LLC and hold the title of business assets in the business name. That way they have no personal liability and can take full advantage of any deductions allowed. While this puts them in a better position when it comes to liability and taxes, it may not be the best position. The specialized private trust I'm referring to is federally regulated under the Universal Trust Code (UTC), which supersedes state law. If an LLC holding your assets is a good move, then a federally regulated trust that supersedes state law is a great move. That's why you want to choose the federally regulated trust for asset protection as well as other benefits.

Not only do taxes follow title, but so does liability. If you're in real estate and accustomed to putting investment properties into LLCs, that's "good protection." If there's a "slip and fall," then you are separate from the ownership and cannot be held liable or have any other assets mixed up in a possible lawsuit. That's the common game, correct? What happens if the federal government comes after those assets, though? The IRS is absolutely capable of piercing the corporate veil and getting those assets because federal law supersedes state law. That's why, if given the choice, you want to hold your assets and income in a federally regulated trust for maximum liability protection. This type of specialized private trust is registered with the IRS and has a federal TIN. This type of trust is under federal jurisdiction, so if you were to sue this trust, you'd have to do it in federal court, not state court. Good luck finding a federally licensed tax or trust attorney. Prosecuting attorneys are different, but tax, trust, and estate attorneys can't touch this stuff. This is the "great" option because it protects your assets from lawsuits, creditors, judgments, divorces, etc. Don't play the game that others play at the state LLC level.

If you do not own something, you are not liable for it. This does not mean that there is no liability, though. If your trust owns a real estate property, and somebody slips and falls on the property, they can't sue you. They can sue the trust, though. In this case, they would only have access to the assets in that trust. If you separate assets from each other through other entities, you isolate and protect them. They would not be able to sue you personally because you do not have ownership of the property.

You may have heard references to this type of specialized private trust during the 2012 election. When Republican nominee Mitt Romney was asked about his tax returns, he said everything was in a "blind trust," and claimed he did not know what was in that trust. He was referring to the 1041 specialized private trust. He has given up ownership of all of his assets and incomes to various trusts so that they cannot be subject to scrutiny by anyone. In fact, trusts are considered a separate "person" by law. They have a separate identity, and nobody has any right to look at or understand what's in them. The privacy clauses in these trust contracts are so iron clad that the assets cannot be entered into a court of law unless, of course, the specific trust has done something criminal, in which case it may be challenged for obvious reasons. Imagine you were sued for something, such as divorce, for example. If the other party is not part of the trust, the judge may view the trust in chambers to verify the privacy and protection clauses, then he or she would be required to not allow the trust to be entered into court. This foundation of privacy, like the rest of the trust structure, is backed up by Supreme Court precedent.

Protecting your assets

I've given you a lot to think about, and I'm sure you have a lot of questions. Before you read on, take some time to pause and reflect on the following questions as they relate to your business or personal economy. If you are examining your personal economy, it's important that you are familiar with the protections set up around it. If you lack certain protections, you could be risking everything you have.

- How much protection do your assets and income have from lawsuits?
- What are you doing to protect your wealth from inflation?
- Do you have a strategy to keep your money growing and outpacing inflation, no matter what the markets are doing?
- Is your wealth and money growing independently from the markets and your otherassets?
- Do you have protection against everything that can erode your wealth?
- How are you protecting your business, assets, and incomes from taxation, inflation, interest, lawsuits, and divorce?

Most of my clients admit that their assets have very little, or no, protection. Some say they have no idea how to protect their assets. If you're feeling perplexed, that's normal. I'm not trying to trick you or make you feel inadequate about your personal economy. My goal is to pique your interest and make you curious enough to learn about the changes you can make to secure your personal economy.

I often meet business owners who don't realize that liability also follows ownership and title. It's simple, though. If you own all of your stuff, you're liable for it. Hopefully this never happens, but that also means that everything can be taken away, including your business. Most CPAs and attorneys tell you that the solution is to put your business in an LLC. However, that may not hold up in court because an

LLC may be considered a disregarded entity. That means that the government could pierce the corporate veil, or you may be subjected to judgments, creditors, etc. The type of specialized private trust I help my clients set up is under federal jurisdiction and is protected from government entities and other entities, such as the IRS (unless there is illegal activity and the trust comes under scrutiny, for obvious reasons).

The questions about inflation baffle a lot of my new clients. They either won't have an answer, or they'll tell me their strategy is to buy silver and gold. The problem with that strategy is that the government can kick the can down the road for a very long time before your investment pays off. Look at Japan, for example. That country has been hyper inflating the yen for four decades now. If you're waiting for precious metals to make you rich, you never know when that day may come. It becomes a timing game, just like bitcoin or anything like that.

When I see inflation starting to happen, I move my cash into businesses or income-producing assets. I look for something that is producing a revenue or dividend, such as life insurance. If the dollar is strong, or assets like real estate are going down in value, you want your money to be in dollars in case there is a crash. That's when life insurance would come into play. One option is just to hold your cash in life insurance and earn the dividends (which is real money coming into your account) because the dividends paid often beat inflation. Your other option is to deploy that capital into productive assets, such as real estate, land, or other businesses. After all, if inflation is driving those up, then you're also beating inflation. You can hedge everything with your life insurance policy acting as part of your "corpus," and as a central operating account that can be growing in your trust.

If you don't know how much protection your assets have, then you will continue to leak money throughout your lifetime. Every dollar you don't capture and control will add up and cost you a fortune over time. For example, if you are 40-years old, making $200,000 per year, and expecting to increase that by inflation (3%), then by the time you turn 65, your income potential will be $7,291,853. If you had $150,000 in a guaranteed account, such as a specialized private trust, which earns

Wealth and Income Potential

Current Age	40
Retirement Age	65
Current Income	$200,000
Income Growth	3%
Current Savings	$150,000
Investment Return	6%

At your retirement age of 65, your income potential will be $7,291,853 and your wealth potential will be $16,176,970.

uninterrupted compound interest, it grows to $16,176,970! When I ask clients how they have things structured, and which mechanisms they use to keep all their money, they typically look at me like deer in the headlights. Their shock continues to grow when I show them the numbers I just mentioned. These are "legacy" numbers. This is how you create a legacy that will grow from generation to generation and help hundreds of thousands of people.

Those numbers are easier to look at than what you would see if you were not keeping and growing these dollars. You probably don't want to see what happens when you leak out tax dollars to Uncle Sam, but I'm going to show you anyway. Using the same scenario as above, assuming a top tax rate of 37%, you would have lost $5,436,616 from age 40 to 65! That's insane, but what's worse is that those dollars are gone and lost forever. You'll never be able to invest them back into your business, or grow that wealth and see returns. It's just gone. What is it going to cost you if you decide not to focus on keeping that money? If you think that is the right thing to do as far as your family and charitable giving is concerned, then I suggest you write a check today for the $5,436,616 and send it to the IRS. Rip the bandage off, and just pay them upfront. Nobody will stop you.

Let's take this deeper. On average, we tend to carry approximately 34% debt-to-income ratio. That means after taxes, on every dollar we bring in, we typically pay an additional 34 cents on each dollar to service our debt (credit cards, student loans, car loans, home loans, business loans, etc.). Between leaking out taxes and debt service, that's an astronomical $10,717,900! Can you imagine keeping that money, growing that wealth, and multiplying it into perpetuity? We could help a lot of foster children with that kind of philanthropic capital.

Wealth Potential vs. Expenditures

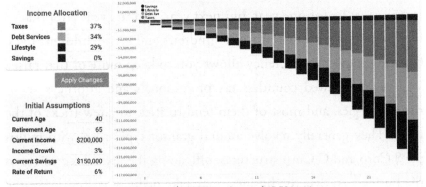

Savings: $643,781   Spent: $15,533,189

The rest of your income and money typically goes to expenses and overhead—your personal economy. The average American business owner or entrepreneur spends between 20-40% of every dollar after tax on living expenses, such as food, fuel, clothing, entertainment, and travel. If you hit that in the middle, and take just 30% from the rest of the money going through your personal economy, there goes the rest of your wealth!

The key to winning this game is to reverse the flow of your wealth. You must allocate every dollar that comes into your personal economy in a way that maximizes your potential growth in order to have more resources to help others. When you can do this and couple it with a solid mission, your world view will change. Your self-view will change. Your life will become something that you've only dreamed about, and your legacy will make people proud.

Tax efficiency

Tax efficiency is one of the most important keys to long-term success. Imagine giving yourself a 30% raise right now. How much would that be, and what would you do with the money you were able to keep? It won't just be for one year, but next year, and the year after that—into perpetuity throughout your children's and grandchildren's lives. Creating more tax efficiency allows you to keep more of that raise.

I've interviewed countless tax professionals and attorneys about their strategies, and most of them tend to stick to a few tricks of the trade. They generally revolve around grantor type trusts with multiple S Corp and C Corp structures, offloading the tax consequences to the business so that the business may take deductions and lower the ultimate tax rate. The lower the tax rate, the better position you put yourself in to create tax efficiency. If you hide the money, and spend the excess on things you may not need, or things you may not want, you lower the ultimate tax rate to maybe 15-20% as the effective rate.

What if you didn't have to spend the money to create a deduction? You could increase your bottom line, become more profitable, lower your overhead, expenses, and deductions. That would have a major impact on your overall wealth. Forget the 30% raise I mentioned earlier. What if you were given 30-40% more income and you got to keep all of it? This becomes confusing in the 1040 system because you have to use every play in the book, pull out every weapon in your arsenal, hide your money, and literally report less income in order to pay less tax.

Everyone is equal under the law. In the United States, that's the gold standard. Contract law supersedes all the other laws of the land. These principles, or rules, date back hundreds of years before the foundation of America in 1776. These principles are based on British Common Law, and they date back to the 1500s. The law is there to protect us all, not just the elite few. If you know the law, then you can play the same game as the billionaires and live a similar life. If politicians write the law, including tax law, and expect you to follow that law, then they can't write separate laws for themselves. That would be illegal. Instead, they write laws that they can take advantage of (along with their wealthy donors) and then they write laws that the masses are supposed to follow. Congress originally created the IRS to collect tax for one year, on incomes of $20,000 or more. That's the equivalent of $480,000 today. Very few members of the working class fit that bill. The typical small family business, or individual entrepreneur, didn't make that kind of money back then, so they were not expected to pay.

The Federal Reserve

A secret gathering on a secluded island laid the foundation for the Federal Reserve System. I can't make this stuff up, and all the information is on federalreservehistory.org. In November 1910, six men met at the Jekyll Island Club off the coast of Georgia with the intent of creating a plan to reform the nation's banks. The participants (Nelson Aldrich, A. Piatt Andrew, Henry Davison, Arthur Shelton, Frank Vanderlip, and Paul Warburg) kept everything so secretive that they didn't even admit to holding the meeting for more than 20 years. The Jekyll Island Club had very exclusive membership, and it is likely that John Pierpont Morgan (commonly known as J.P.), or another influential member of the wealthy elite, set up the meeting. Other notable members included Marshall Field and William Kissam Vanderbilt, whose "mansion-sized 'cottages' dotted the island," according to the web site. The club was described as "the richest, the most exclusive, the most inaccessible" club in the world by *Munsey's Magazine* circa 1904.

At the time, the wealthy elite were in position to seize control of the nation's wealth, and that's exactly what they did. The meeting set the stage to form an alliance with Congress, which passed the Federal Reserve Act in 1913. This established the need to collect tax from producers in order to repay money borrowed by the U.S. Treasury. When Congress passed the bill, the tax code that we still use today began to take shape. Politicians made sure the tax code was specific, but that it left plenty of room for their wealthy financiers to legally offset, or keep, everything they made. The new rules of the game were largely kept secret by the political class and wealthy elite.

This may sound shady, and you have every right to be upset. However, you also have every right to take advantage of the same rules. Like I mentioned earlier, the law is designed to protect all citizens of the United States, not just a certain class or group. That means you, too. You only need to make one simple (but not easy) decision to shift your mindset, level up your skill set, and structure your personal economy using the 1041 trust and foundation system. Think about everything you own and what bank accounts your wealth and income hit. I want you to clearly see who owns that income and those assets.

I have a client in Colorado who spent his entire career building a dental practice from the ground up. He contacted me after he hit a wall while planning for his retirement. He didn't have much saved up because everything that came in seemed to be going right back out to pay taxes, bills, and debt. He had been paying his ex-wife alimony and child support for about 15 years.

Part of their divorce decree stated that when he sold his practice, she would get half of the sale price. Additionally, their two daughters had graduated from college and he was responsible for the student loan debt, which was more than $200,000. He had been trying to figure out the most efficient way to pay off that debt and still be able to retire. Originally, we made a retirement plan that called for him to work another 10 years. A few years later, though, he was mentally ready to retire.

He had been trying to sell his practice for two years and nobody had even bid. At the time, it was difficult to get a loan to purchase a business. New dentists were already saddled with undergraduate and graduate student loan debt, so not many were looking to take on even more debt to purchase a practice. It was a difficult environment for anyone in the medical field who wanted to exit the business, retire, and walk away. He had been slashing his asking price consistently for two years to the point that it was almost down 50%.

I had already helped him set up trusts and foundations. Since nobody was even looking at buying the practice, I suggested that he sell his business to his business trust for the current market value. He figured out what his type of practice had been selling for in his area and wrote up a contract between himself and his business trust to complete the sale. He gave his ex-wife 50% and considered the deal done.

The single overarching premise for everything in the tax code is about ownership. If you own stuff, you're taxed on it. Whoever owns things is taxed according to the code. Different entities are taxed differently, according to the code. Different entities are independent "actors," or "people," according to the law.

My client's ex-wife became suspicious of how much she received from the sale of his practice. His attorney asked him who owned the trust, and he called me in a panic. I was so stunned that I questioned his attorney's expertise and license. In order to get a license to practice family law, you must understand the ownership of assets, who owns which assets, and how those assets might be bought and sold.

Later, his ex-wife brought him to court and accused him of making a false sale. She claimed that he actually owned the business trust, that he sold the practice to himself, and that the sale was not legitimate. She intended to sue him not only for the amount she thought she was owed, but everything else he had, too. I spoke to my client and his attorney on the phone and explained trusts, contracts, and that ultimately he didn't own anything in that trust. He was the trustee, and his sole responsibility, per the contract, was for the financial betterment of the trust, on behalf of the beneficiaries. That's it. Since he did not own anything, it was not for his betterment or benefit.

Once he truly wrapped his mind around that concept, he was able to walk confidently into a meeting between both parties and their attorneys. When he was asked who owned the trust, he was ready. "Nobody," he responded. "Nobody owns it. Here is the EIN number. It's registered with the federal government. You can research it yourself.

There is no owner, the trust is its own independent entity viewed as a person by law. It was a legally binding sale, per the contract."

That was it, case closed. Nothing happened after that. He walked away with everything, yet he still paid his wife the agreed upon amount, even though he had no financial responsibility to do so.

Divorce is simply a lawsuit between two people. As such, each party must disclose all of their personal assets. A family trust, however, is a completely separate person, or entity. It has nothing to do with my friend, his ex-wife, or their divorce. It would be no different than his ex-wife asking you to disclose all of your assets to her just because you know her ex-husband. She has no right to look at any assets that you own or have them enter the court. It's that simple.

The law is straightforward about ownership, taxes, and liability. However, there is a gray area for grantor type trusts and statutory trusts in general. Often times, the trustee of those trusts is an attorney friend of the grantor, so the relationship could potentially be illegitimate. That's not the case with a federally regulated specialized private trust, though, because you don't have any ownership interest in the assets. You do not have any ownership of the trust, so you do not have any ownership of the income or money going into the trust. There are major differences in liability and taxability between statutory and federal trusts. Make sure your tax guru knows what they are talking about.

How to avoid burnout

As you move forward in this process, you will need to align the goals you have for your personal economy with a cause you are passionate about. When your talents, passions, values, and beliefs work with your financial goals, something else is going to happen. You're going to lead under these characteristics, and people will tell you that "you've changed." They may also tell you all the work you've done is a lie, and that's not who you are. They will want you to believe a different story.

All of this negativity may cause some hard times, and you may forget who you've become through this process. I spent three years having conversations with myself about my purpose. Three years! There were no cheerleaders telling me I was on the right path. Nobody coached me or championed my success. It was just me trying to find my way through a pit of darkness. I know now though, with absolute certainty, that the daily focus of reaching for the light, moving forward, giving, helping, and loving on others is a powerful way to live.

If you can't power through tough times and truly feel your purpose, I guarantee you will burn out. Your life will revert to how it was before you started this journey. I have seen this happen to hundreds of families who have come so far in this process only to hit a rough patch and cancel everything out.

The only thing that allows anyone to grow and become more aware of anything significant is a deep-rooted commitment to purpose. If you lack purpose, I promise that you will fall from the top of your game into a state of depression. You will be rising to the peak of having it all, hit abundance, and then you will self-sabotage. You'll burn it all down to the ground just like I did and just like so many people did before me.

This book is not a manual that you can bury on a shelf after you've completed it. This is a lifestyle that requires you to study for the rest of your life. Don't let a scarcity mindset hold you back. Keep working to shift your mindset, level up your skill set, and find true prosperity. There is no other answer than to keep moving forward. I'm not arrogant enough to believe that you wouldn't have found your way without this book. The process looks different for everyone. I can't prescribe the exact process for you, but I can help lead you to a space where you can find abundance and true prosperity, if you want it.

I have nothing without my purpose. I am a chronically living human who pretends that my life actually matters, yet hollow inside my soul no matter how empty or full my bank account may be. Without my purpose, I would be left with the same hollow feeling no matter how drunk, high, or sober I got. I'd be left with hopelessness. This is why most people pursue mediocrity and surround themselves with people who say they are awesome. That's the easy way.

My wish for you is that you'll be bold, and live up to the gifts and talents you've been given, so that you may help others while fulfilling your ultimate purpose. A purpose-driven lifestyle is not for everyone, and that's OK. Are you ready to live this life of meaning and purpose, and touch on the ability to have it all? I'm talking about every area of your life: health, fitness, relationships, connections, business, bank accounts, and income. Imagine a life where you are able to "have it all" through making one simple choice.

When I reflect on my family's journey, I recognize patterns and habits that I wish could have been different. I desire to go back, collapse time, and pull this off so much faster. In 2008, when my wife and I got married and started our journey in foster care, we struggled to figure out our purpose. We didn't know where to focus our time, resources, or talents. While we discovered our passion for helping kids heal from life's hurts, we didn't have the resources we needed to pull this off. I was struggling with my business. I didn't know how to handle overhead, accounting, employees, payroll, taxes, investments, insurance, etc. My hope was in keeping more money, growing my wealth, and giving back aggressively. I also saw that the tax system we were participating in was flawed and wouldn't allow us to live how we wanted.

As I've mentioned, 62 cents on every dollar earned is already accounted for in some kind of tax. We pay taxes on things we buy, sell, own, on the money we make, give, and every step in between. It is insane! The average business owner and entrepreneur has to work longer, harder hours just to be able to pay typical expenses. After Uncle Sam takes off his chunk of flesh, there is very little left over to save for the future or to even think about giving back.

That is the dilemma American entrepreneurs face, but we can change that. You can change that for yourself, your family, your future posterity, and generations to come. You can break the chain in the cycle of slavery to taxes and become a light in the darkness. The decision I made was simple. I committed more than a decade ago to help children in the foster care system and parents who have adopted kids from that system. It's a simple mission, but it has a profound ripple effect on our society. These kids, who feel unwanted, unloved, and unworthy, don't deserve to feel that way. No child does! We all have value, and we are all here for a reason. It's up to us to discover our unique mission and purpose, then to live that out in a massive way!

During the next chapter, you will discover things you never thought about pertaining to your family, values, and beliefs. It's not just crucial to figure out your passions, but your family's passions, as well. Don't skip over this. This is the good part of life. Sit down with your children and grandchildren and have deep discussions about meaning and purpose. That is how connections are solidified, relationships are made, experiences are shared, and joy is magnified.

"I learned from my dad that change and experimentation are constants and important. You have to keep trying new things."

- S. Robson Walton,
son of Walmart founder Sam Walton

CHAPTER THREE
DISRUPT THE SYSTEM

Sometimes being a business owner and entrepreneur can be a lonely experience, yet once upon a time in America, it was the norm. We were farmers, shopkeepers, butchers, bakers, and street vendors trying to eke out an existence. We created our own wealth, built a life for our families, and worked hard to leave a legacy.

Ownership is a founding principle of the United States. Freedom and ownership go hand in hand. When you work for someone else, you don't own the results since you produced them for someone else. They own your production. When your production no longer matters, you're no longer a free person. Working for someone else stifles creativity, the expansion of ideas, and so much growth potential. This goes back to the principles on which our country was founded: freedom, ownership, and sovereignty. It is spelled out clearly in the constitution that the government is the agent and you are the principal. The government should work for you because you are sovereign and at the highest point in the hierarchy.

Not many business owners or W2 employees feel that way, though. That's why when you make the shift to the 1041 system, you can play a different game and take back control and ownership of your life, freedom, and liberty. If you want to live a free life, you can't play by the rules everyone else follows because those have been corrupted. Giving up ownership of your possessions is a Biblical principle. Mark 8:36 (NLT) asks "what do you benefit if you gain the whole world but lose your own soul?" Abundance is another Biblical principle. In The Parable of the Bags of Gold in Matthew Chapter 25, Jesus describes a man who entrusts his wealth to his servants before leaving on a journey. When he returns, the master responds to the servants who put their bags of gold to work and doubled them by saying "Well done, good and faithful servant! You have been faithful with a few things; I will put you in charge of many things. Come and share your master's happiness!" Jesus concludes the parable by summarizing the lesson to be learned: "For whoever has will be given more, and they will have an abundance."

It's sad that it has only taken 100 years and change (since the foundation of the Federal Reserve System) to corrupt the foundation of our country. We've given away our sovereignty and become slaves to our government due to taxes. This is a hard truth to learn, but it explains why Americans seem to have lost the ambition to produce, create, and grow. I will go into much greater detail on this point when I talk about the rule of 97 in Chapter Eight.

If you've lost your ambition to produce, who can blame you? You've been told so many lies by Wall Street and the government. Some people even equate being a business owner to being a crook or a thug. Look at how people view billionaires such as Bill Gates and Jeff Bezos. Anyone who has truly excelled in business gets labeled by others. The wealthiest Americans have private foundations that have achieved so much good for the world. However, instead of praising wealthy business owners for all the great things they've done in the world, people assume that they cheated along their path to success or got a leg up because they were born into wealth.

There are people who believe business owners are so greedy that it's OK to take an owner's wealth and give it to others. They try to devalue business owners, marketing to us as if we don't know what is best for our own companies. They don't know you, though, or the sacrifices you've made. They don't know the countless hours you've spent awake at night stressing about how you're going to take care of your people. They don't know how much you worry about running your business while dealing with overhead, expenses, taxes, insurance, and payroll. You're the one who has built a business and finally living the life you've worked so hard for, and now you're getting criticized for your efforts. Once you are successful, it feels as if people either think you know someone with insider knowledge or that you must have done something wrong to get what you have.

The problem is that people who don't know the first thing about you are willing to pass judgment on you. Business owners are often alone. I've sat down and listened to bankers, advisors, and joker brokers try to tell me what to do with my money. Yet, I can't stop wondering why they think they know more about my business than I do? They usually tell me to do the exact opposite of what I've been doing for almost 20 years. I keep hearing that I would be wise to take my money and invest it in someone else's company, or that it makes sense to put my money into their accounts. I'm the one who has built my business and created the profits, yet that doesn't matter to them. When I take a step back, I recognize the only things that are going to last are myself and my investments, which is why I invest in me, my businesses, and my strategies.

Business owners and entrepreneurs are the new common enemy to large financial institutions and the government because they both want to control the flow of money. Politicians have systematically allowed Wall Street to grow into a $2.5 trillion per year behemoth over the last 70 years. A lot of money exchanged hands in shady deals, and so-called "watchdog groups" turned their heads. For example, during the financial crisis in 2008-09, the bond rating agencies all gave mortgage-backed securities (sub-prime mortgages) AAA ratings. It turns out, those agencies were getting paid by the firms that were selling the MBS to rate their products as "super safe" investments when they obviously were not.

This is another truth that is tough to swallow, yet it motivates those of us who know we are the No. 1 asset in our own personal economies. We must protect our production with everything we have. Without us, there is no production, growth, income, or wealth. Your first priority should be to protect that mechanism of production for your family and legacy. Likewise, there is no investment outside of yourself and your business that will get you where you want to go. There is no magical formula, no magical investment, no magical ATM outside of your business—not bitcoin, real estate, or any other "safe bet." In fact, there are few true investments today. Putting your money in the stock market, which is pure speculation, is no different than taking it to a casino and playing the odds. What's even worse is that when you accept speculation instead of investing in your business, you're charged endless fees by the company that is supposed to be growing your wealth better than you could.

Wall Street has fed us these lies for more than 70 years. First, you build a business, become successful, and make money. After that, the first thing they'll have you do is take your hard-earned money and hand it over to some broker who will gamble it away in the stock market. They see no value in having you keep, protect, and invest your money back into your No. 1 investment: your business. In fact, they are threatened by that and have spent billions in marketing telling you otherwise. The execs who run Wall Street institutions have foundations and trusts set up in the 1041 system. Yet, they pay employees millions to convince business owners to trust them with their money. They congratulate anyone who has grown to a certain level and literally figured out how to create an ATM that prints money on demand by saying "give me your money and I'll put it to work for you so you can retire." They think they know more about what to do with your money than you do.

Don't be fooled into playing by their rules. There are different principles that are simple to follow, easy to execute, and have been around for generations. Unfortunately, they've been lost to hard-working business owners and entrepreneurs due to the lies of Wall Street and big banks.

The principles I'm talking about are yours to rediscover. They have been used by my family, and hundreds of thousands of other families across the country, to protect what we've built, grow our wealth, and create a legacy. These principles are secrets kept by the wealthiest families in history, politicians, professional athletes, and celebrities. These families have last names like Rockefeller, Kennedy, Hilton, and more recently Gates, Buffet, Zuckerberg, and Bezos. The rules of this game have been passed around by the wealthy elite for more than a century, handed down for generations. In fact, they've been hidden in plain sight and kept just out of reach from successful business owners and entrepreneurs like you. I have spoken to business owners who say these principles aren't right for them, and that's fine. What I'm teaching you about is definitely not something you would hear under the tutelage of advisors like Dave Ramsey or Wall Street talking heads. If you were to go to a dinner party with wealthy politicians and their financial benefactors, though, this would be common knowledge and practice.

If you build a business and witness it burn to the ground, like I have, that's going to force a shift in you. When you see early success, it's no wonder you think the "road goes on forever, and the party never ends." At some point, though, you come to the sober realization that everything you've built can only get you so far. The more money you make, the more taxes you pay, and you start to see the point of diminishing returns. More success comes with more resistance in the form or taxation and legislation. Not only can the government tax you to death, but they can change the laws at will, too. In 2020, during the COVID-19 pandemic, 80% of California restaurants permanently shut their doors due to shutdowns and restrictions on indoor dining. At one point, California lawmakers allowed outdoor dining if certain specifications were met. So, thousands of restaurant owners invested a fortune in improving and expanding outdoor seating options only to have the government decide that any services except carryout and delivery had to be shut down once again.

I know that the 1041 world of private foundations and specialized private trusts isn't for everyone. If you're happy with your current situation, then keep doing what you're doing. However, if you're not content, you may have to shift some paradigms.

The scarcity mindset serves you no purpose. In order to expand into abundance, in order to build true wealth and prosperity, you must become a different person. If that sounds harsh, it should. If you knew exactly how to achieve your wildest dreams for your life, then you probably wouldn't be reading this book. You would have already set up your family, business, and charitable trusts and foundations. Setting these up will allow you to stop bleeding your tax dollars. In turn, you would be able to give back in a massive way because of this intentional structure and your new "operating system."

"I want to disrupt giving."

That is how I described my mission to Rob Siracusano, who I trained and competed with on the national diving team for 10 years, as he lamented how much money he paid in taxes every year. I said it with a straight face, but he laughed anyway. His business had seen astronomical growth, but the government had been taking millions of dollars from it annually and he had no cure. He had been extremely generous during his parabolic rise and came up with his own system for giving to causes he wanted to support. Rob has been able to give millions back to charities, including the sport we both loved, but he felt as if he were lighting money on fire when he paid taxes.

He was one of the smartest guys I knew in finance. *Forbes* listed him as one of the top 50 wealth advisors in the country, and he currently manages more than $1 billion in assets. The firm he started from nothing now tops $700 million a year in revenue. He pays an army of tax, estate planning, and statutory trust attorneys to hide his money and reduce his tax burden. Everything he had was still in the 1040 tax system, though, not the 1041. As a result, it cost him personally more than $10 million in the last five years alone. Can you imagine what would be possible with that amount of philanthropic capital? That's exactly what nagged him.

"Why don't you just write a check to Uncle Sam right now for the next 10 years? Get it over with," I said. "Just rip the bandage off and send the check so Congress can use it to repay some of our federal debt."

In response, he used some choice words to basically get me to shut up and help him. So, I walked him through the entire 1041 trust and foundation system and then introduced him to a federally licensed Enrolled Agent.

> "I WANT TO DISRUPT GIVING."
> - SEAN BRISCOMBE

Even though Rob had been so successful for so long, and surrounded himself with the best accountants and attorneys money could buy, he still didn't know about the 1041 system. It took him a while to warm up to the idea of giving up ownership of his assets, and setting up foundations and trusts, but he is currently trying to get things lined up. Not only does he have to convince his state-licensed legal team, but he also has to make sure he stays in compliance with the SEC.

It bugged me that he didn't even know about the 1041 system before our conversations, though. That was a huge "a-ha" moment for me. The fundamental truth that I learned from this is that just because you're successful, that doesn't mean you know everything. The more I studied this system, and consulted with the best practitioners in the country, the more I realized that the wealthiest families play by a completely different set of rules. They can choose to live a purpose- driven lifestyle on a daily basis because of their ability to keep their money, grow their wealth, and generously give more of what they grow.

I believe that we are all equal under the law, and that the law exists to protect every citizen of this country. The United States does not have different sets of laws for different groups of people. That is how I realized that if I can learn this system and apply it to my life, then I can help others do the same thing. I decided to start making simple choices in my personal economy to affect positive change. If I can keep more of my money, and create more growth, then I can generate more philanthropic capital for children in the foster community.

"I'm coming to this world not to work. I want to come to this world to enjoy my life. I don't want to die in my office. I want to die on the beaches."

- Jack Ma, Chinese business magnate

CHAPTER FOUR
PREPARE FOR THE JOURNEY

We will continue to learn the key strategies and concepts of the 1041 trust and foundation system later in this book. First, though, we have to go back to the beginning. You've probably heard somebody tell you "if you don't know where you're going, any path will take you there." The same is true for your legacy and the future of your family. If you don't have a clear vision of your current situation and what you ultimately want, then you need to take a step back to develop that picture first. You need a tangible path with measurable outcomes so that you know what you are setting out to accomplish.

Our work begins with your mindset. You're going to learn about how your mind creates different frames, and how your life operates within those frames, which will add power to your perspective. After that, you'll be ready to define your purpose, which brings us to your "why" question. When I started teaching people about the 1041 system years ago, I realized I had been doing a lot of work without answering the "why" question for myself, yet.

For years, I thought my purpose in life was to win a gold medal diving for Team U.S.A. in the Olympics. After I accomplished that,

I would leverage my medal to accumulate wealth, which would then (and only then) put me in a position to help people other than myself. I was on track to compete in the 1992 Olympics Trials and, hopefully, make the team to compete in Barcelona until I injured my wrist and had to have surgery. One of my teammates, Scott Donie, went on to win a silver medal in Barcelona, while I watched the competition on TV with my wrist in a cast. That was a dark time in my life, and I decided to quit diving. After I recovered, though, several coaches and divers talked me into training for the '96 Olympics in Atlanta. I ended up moving to Austin to work with the Olympic coach, Matt Scoggin, fell in love with the place and made it my home. Ultimately, I ended up back on the national team and trained, traveled, and competed with the group before the Atlanta games.

When my Olympic dreams ended, I struggled to come up with the "why?" for my new stage of life. I left my job as a physical therapist so I could focus on diving. While I trained for the Olympics, I worked at Home Depot and was groomed to be a store manager as part of the company's Olympic Job Opportunities Program. It was a great gig with amazing stock options and bonuses for managers, but it came with all the headaches of any retail job. I worked early mornings, late nights, weekends, and holidays. Eventually, I left for a higher paying job with Dell, which was expanding rapidly. A former employee of mine at Home Depot who ended up at Dell gave them my name when he heard they were looking for great managers and leaders. At Dell, I put all of my money into stock options, which split and doubled every year. After three years, I left to join a small team that founded Mall.com. We ended up selling that business for a large sum of money and splitting it five ways. We then made the decision to go all in with what we made and started another internet company right before the dot-com bubble burst in the early 2001. That was the first loss of my business career, and it hurt.

I was forced to hit the reboot button on my career and start all over again. This time, I got into real estate lending and investing. I am 100% self-taught when it comes to banking and finance. In fact, the only formal higher education courses I've ever taken in finance were continuing education classes for my licenses. My teachers, mentors, and coaches are all business owners and entrepreneurs themselves. They are elite-level hedge fund managers and some of the brightest financial minds of our time. I've been blessed to have known these leaders in the industry, and I've studied their business decisions for almost two decades now. Eventually, I became successful in the field and ran my own businesses. Some would say that I had a lot of luck in my business career. However, I would say that I simply applied the knowledge I learned as a diver to what I do in business. I set huge targets, had a solid work ethic, and learned to be disciplined enough to focus on one desired outcome. If I didn't hit my target the first time, I knew how to course correct and put in the work necessary to get it the next time.

The more I would hustle and grind, the more money I made. That felt great! What bothered me, though, was that every time I made more money, I would have to give a bigger and bigger chunk to Uncle Sam. After working long hours, investing back into my business, and taking care of my employees, paying taxes felt like a punishment.

This can cause business owners to become stingy with the money left over after taxes. I believed in tithing to my church home, but I wasn't the most faithful in that discipline. The challenge business owners and entrepreneurs have is how to allocate what's left after the tithe. Where should it go?

While I became successful in my life after diving, I still felt lost when it came to my purpose and legacy. These were blanks I wanted to fill in so badly that I attended experiential workshops to help answer my "why" questions. My breakthrough moment didn't come until I joined Wake Up Warrior, Garret J. White's coaching program in Laguna Beach, California. This program specifically targets married business men with children, and it is designed to wake them up so they can live with purpose and meaning. The first stage strategically beats you up physically, mentally, and emotionally in order to strip away your fears, anxieties, and the lies you've been telling yourself. I spent my time in intense workouts, journaling, and meditation sessions so I could be liberated from all of the negative baggage swirling in my head. Once I was free of those emotions, I could focus on what I wanted to achieve.

I had started to learn about trusts, foundations, and the 1041 system around the time I joined Warrior. The program's ultimate goal is for participants to achieve true prosperity, go beyond abundance, and become focused on contribution. It clicked in my head that the 1041 system was the missing link I had been searching for in my life. My passion was helping children in the foster care system, and my purpose was to teach others how to set up private trusts and foundations to further the causes that made them passionate. The Warrior program taught me that before you can lead others to something, you have to learn it and live it first. I knew I had to learn as much as I could about the 1041 system, prove I could give up ownership of my possessions, and become a giving leader. Only then could I live out my purpose of helping others set up foundations and become giving leaders, as well.

Discovering your purpose

In the next chapter, there will be some tough questions that you have to answer honestly if you want to truly transform your life and help others. The goal is to get you to reflect on the core areas of your life. Purpose has a simple definition: the reason something exists. Everyone has a purpose, some are just trickier to identify. To understand your purpose, you need to understand your vision.

How did you get where you are today? This may sound hokey to anyone who has built a successful business. After all, you got where you are through hard work, commitment, help from friends and family, and some luck along the way. That's not what I'm talking about, though. In the beginning you had a vision (whether clear or murky) for success. Now, maybe your vision was to enrich your family, take vacations, and provide for your loved ones. Those are noble things, don't get me wrong. As a husband and father, I can attest to the deep need to provide for my little girls and my beautiful bride. My vision is to create something bigger for my life, though.

I want to build something that will outlast my wife and me, our daughters, and even our grandkids. I desire something that can grow from generation to generation and accomplish something great along the way. To define my own dreams, I had to "re-imagine" what it looked like to grow and scale a business. Once you allow your mindset to shift from scarcity to abundance, you stop stressing about survival because you can focus your whole budget on something bigger and better. Making a positive impact on the world is a huge component of true prosperity.

Maybe you've felt your calling already. If so, then congratulations, you're among an elite group of giving leaders who is ready to take the next step toward a life of purpose and meaning. In fact, you can skip the rest of this chapter, if you so choose.

If you're still searching, congratulations to you, too! The uncertainty you're feeling is a normal part of the human experience. Let's get clear about where you are today. That's the only way to determine what you really want, why that matters to you, and how to proceed.

Everything that exists today was manifested, produced, created, and driven by purpose. You must examine your soul and determine what awakens it. That's your purpose, and you will soon be using it to write your own mission statement. This process will walk you through four distinct categories: your passions, unique abilities, values, and beliefs. Think of these categories like the corners of a blanket with your mission statement laying in the middle of it. If I were to reach down and grab the middle of that blanket, all four corners would come along. Your mission statement will be the foundation that, when you pull on it, brings a series of conversations with it.

After that is written, you'll use it to develop your family's declaration statement, which will unite your loved ones for generations along a path of building, growing, and giving. My wife and I came up with this one for our family using the same process:

"To the abused, abandoned, the broken-hearted, and the ones who have no one in their corner. Know that your long nights are coming to an end. We are on our way to help you heal from life's hurts."

Your mission statement will help you maintain focus day in and day out. It will fuel your day-to-day activity, weekly focal points, monthly milestones, quarterly targets, and lifelong expansion. It's the calling that comes from your gut and what you were born to do.

There are some fundamental truths you must live by to have this type of lifestyle. The first is commitment. What will you tell people who think this system is crazy? This process is a journey, not a destination. You will have people who doubt what you're doing. You've got to remain mission-focused, knock off specific targets, and shift your mindset in order to become this new person.

I focus on what I believe is crucial for success in my personal economy: transformation and shift. The biggest transformation and shift you will begin to go through is from growth to contribution. When we shift from focusing solely on ourselves, and our own growth, to contributing to and helping others, then we shift our energy from making, keeping, and growing money to giving back in a more meaningful way. When you're transforming from a life of scarcity to abundance, being able to stabilize that abundance is the first step. If you don't feel like you are in a position to have stabilized abundance, I would be happy to cover that with you personally. However, that's not something this book will focus on. We're going to focus on the growth it takes to go from abundance to true prosperity. This will allow you to feel more confident and operate from a position of power, certainty, and clarity. Without those elements, our brains can't function correctly, and we won't be able to make decisions that will positively affect generations.

Sometimes I lose commitment from potential clients before the process even begins because they don't feel gifted enough in the area that makes them passionate. Hard work and passion are a great pair, though. As a diver, I had a knack for flipping and twisting, along with incredible spatial awareness. By the time I was eight, I was under the tutelage of Rick Schavone, who was Stanford University's head diving coach for more than 40 years, and trained alongside the college athletes (again, something that the NCAA allowed then). I trained every day except Sunday until I was 14, often multiple times a day. I craved being around other athletes who pushed me, supported me, and who I could pour into. I believe that when we pour into others, there is an energy and power that fills us up.

That's why I began to coach while I competed. By the time I turned 10, Stanford divers consistently asked me to observe them. I had a good eye, and I could communicate complex physics and aerodynamics in a straightforward way. The more I coached, the better I became. At 17, I was one of the best technical coaches in the country. My own competitors would approach me at meets for tips. Soon, I was coaching just as much as I was training. I listened to the best coaches in the world from the U.S. Olympic team and loved asking them questions. This helped me become even better at communicating with other athletes about what they needed to do to improve.

I wasn't an expert coach from day one. Everybody starts as a beginner, and this journey is no different. Think about the movie "Catch Me if You Can," starring Leonardo DiCaprio. You don't have to be a subject-matter expert to be able to lead and guide others. Getting involved now, leading with your heart, and serving at the highest possible level will allow you to figure out what works (and what doesn't) for you, your family, and your future.

As your wealth grows in the 1041 trust and foundation system, your mindset will shift from building wealth to contributing acts of service. The more you maximize your ability to give back, the more family, friends, and colleagues will want to follow your lead. Consider it your duty to pass this information on to others who have a heart of service. This is a transformation from production to contribution, which is always more fulfilling than focusing on your own growth. Every day, I ask myself "how can I serve more people?" When you take this to heart, then the contents of this book can completely transform your life, and your business, in ways you never imagined. It is a life-long discipline that takes practice. More importantly, it takes support and a detailed plan.

Everybody's plan will look different. Your blueprint will be customized to your life. It will be a reflection of who you are as a person and who you want to become as a "venture philanthropist." To steal Russel Crowe's line from "Gladiator," one of my favorite movies: "What we do in life echoes in eternity." Keep that in mind as you think through what you want your life to look like.

Your mission and purpose statement

Throughout my career, I have had the privilege of working with thousands of mission- driven people. I've helped ultra-wealthy families who were just starting to focus on philanthropy, and those who have always supported a cause and came to me because they wanted to use their money to do more. I've seen firsthand what works and what mistakes to avoid.

One of my clients is a pilot who emigrated from India. He wanted to give back by helping more students in India have the same educational opportunities that he did, but he was a W2 employee and didn't know the best way to accomplish that. By donating enough of his income to his foundation, he lowered his taxable income below the second threshold. This gave him a huge refund and a $90,000 swing from what he would have paid in taxes to what he could keep and grow. Now he is using that money to set up new schools in his home country.

Another client of mine owns a steel manufacturing business in Oregon. His goal had been to donate $1 million toward fighting hunger in his region. Every year he opens his company's doors to anyone who wants a free Thanksgiving dinner. Recently, he was able to triple what he donated to this cause through what he saved in taxes.

I've also helped people who find themselves in a world of hurt get on the right path.

Sometimes people lack a sense of purpose because they have lost their way. Their compasses are broken. They have no "true north" anymore to guide them in difficult times (or plentiful times). I believe most people suffer from this lack of vision and clarity. It's my experience that those who don't focus on the importance of what they're doing often lose their way and begin to suffer.

Those who maintain a clear focus on who they are, what they're here for, and why that matters, rarely get lost or chase rabbits down impossible holes.

I find it fascinating that most people I meet have a hard time articulating what they really want. When I ask them what they want, I tend to receive blank stares in response, as if they are confused by the question itself. A lot of people that I talk to have never even asked themselves a question like that because it is so hard to answer. I'm not talking about what you want for lunch. I'm not even talking about your career or income. I'm asking about what you truly want out of this experience called life. If we don't ask these questions, we will never benefit from truly expanding or creating anything better than what we already have. Life is expansion. If you're not expanding, growing, learning, and changing, you're not truly living.

We experience life through different inputs. We have a physical body and a spiritual self. We feel accomplishment when we are productive. Yet, in order to be productive, there are four areas of life that must be maintained: your physical body, mind, spirit, and energy. We have to commit to a healthy lifestyle. If your body fails you, it makes it much more difficult to fulfill your purpose. The same goes for your mind, which is why you must protect it from distractions, anxiety, fear, and all the negative influences in our world.

You can't see this any more clearly than on social media. When I lead a client through this process, I recommend that they go on an "information diet." The negative information on social media, or any type of media, is blocking you from fulfilling your mission and purpose. If you're going to create and produce from a position of power, you must have a clear mind.

Whether you pray, journal, read, or whatever it takes, do it daily to feed your mind with good nutrition. This is true for your spirit, too. You must fill it up daily with something that is mission- focused. That's why clarifying your mission and purpose statement will help you stay on track.

Every day, I block off the first two-and-a-half hours for things that help me focus. I exercise and eat something nutritious. I meditate and pray. I journal about insights and revelations I've had. I connect with my wife and children through acts of kindness or writing notes to them. These notes are affirmations of love, honor, and respect. The last thing I do during this time is learn something new related to my field of work and apply it to my day. By doing all of these tasks daily, I am able to feed my purpose, my reason for being here. I am able to create a reality far better than anything I could have dreamed. I am truly able to lead a life of meaning and purpose.

I hope you are beginning to see the power in asking "why." If you can't answer the tough questions, then you need to stop before going any further. Take a step back, breath, relax, and come back with a clear mind.

A mission statement will allow you to create freely. You'll build things you never thought possible while staying energized and focused. It will pull the right people and resources toward you like a magnet. You'll find everything to be so much easier.

As we continue our discussion about the 1041 tax system and how to find your purpose, fund your purpose, and change the world, you will begin to experience life in a whole new way. Your life has always had purpose, meaning, and value. It's up to you to uncover it. You have certain gifts and passions that are unique to you, but you need to leverage them to create a better life for you and your family.

Anything you build starts with the foundation. You must understand the basic building blocks in order to gain clarity about the future. My family and I used the same framework to develop our mission statement. I have led hundreds of families down this path, too, and they have gone on to create their own private foundations. Now, they are giving back more powerfully than anyone thought they could. Through the work you're about to do, you will experience growth and expansion.

If you are not satisfied with your current stage in life, this is often due to a breakdown in your personal economy. There is a conflict between the vision you had for your life and the reality around you. When that gap exists, it causes suffering, stress, anxiety, and fear. We can't operate at our best when our life is painfully hard. It's a struggle just to get through the day without thinking about or acting on distractions. We already discussed distractions caused by social media. Sometimes we are even tempted to sedate ourselves with drugs, alcohol, or any of the multitude of bad habits we form when we're bored or burnt out. Gaining clarity and certainty around your purpose can take away this suffering and get your life back on track.

"It's not hard to make decisions when you know what your values are."

- Roy Disney, co-founder of The Walt Disney Company

CHAPTER FIVE
CRAFTING YOUR MISSION AND PURPOSE STATEMENT

In order to go from abundance to true prosperity, you must first "level-up" and create the person who can actually pull that off. To do that, you have to shatter your worldview, along with your self-view, and rebuild it from a position of power. In this section, we are going to analyze the four quadrants of your mission and purpose to gain clarity about where you stand today. You may either make notes on the four quadrants organizer in the book, or create your own on a piece of paper. Use the following prompts and questions to guide you in this process.

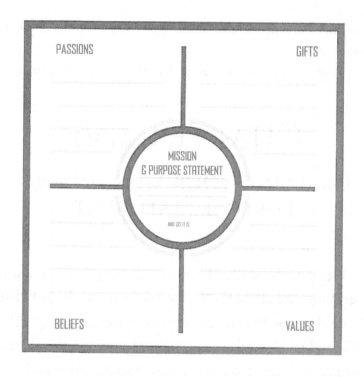

Quadrant 1: Passions

A book I read years ago awakened this piece of my purpose. It's called *The Passion Test*, by Janet and Chris Attwood, and I highly recommend it if you want to take a deeper dive into this topic. *The Passion Test* is simply a series of questions and ideas that are meant to uncover what you are naturally drawn toward. We all have natural abilities and performance levels. Some things come easy, and other things require more work. It's likely that you already participate in some activities that are connected to your passion.

In this quadrant, write your passions, not your goals. Goals are wandering generalities, targets are meaningful specifics. Your passions are the foundation for these targets. If your feet hit the ground in the morning and you are fired up about your to-do list, then you are in perfect alignment with your passions. If you wake up and there is hesitation, fear, anxiety, or depression, then that's a sign from God that you're not in alignment with your passions. Your job may be important when it comes to providing for your family, but it does not help you answer your "why" questions. If you can't answer "why it is important" on that level, it's not a passion.

Make this quadrant into a list, or word jumble, of everything you are passionate about. Use the following questions to guide you if you get stuck, but don't feel like you need to answer all of them.

Questions to consider

- What excites you?
- What do you dream about that makes you wake up on fire?
- How do you enjoy spending your quality time?
- What do you do during your free time?
- What fills you up inside?
- What gives you that power and energy to do things you normally wouldn't do unlessyou were getting paid?
- If money weren't a barrier, what would you do with your time?
- Why do the things you wrote down matter to you?

Quadrant 2: Talents and gifts

Our passions lead us to our talents and gifts. When you imagine a "gift," the image of a wrapped package may enter your mind. Nobody will package and deliver to you what we're talking about in this section, though, because it's something you already have inside you.

These gifts are the talents and strengths that are embedded in the very fabric of your DNA. While we may be able to make ourselves better at some things, what I want you to think about in this quadrant are the things you never had to work hard at to do well. No matter what your situation is, you were born with gifts and talents, so get a pen and write those down. If you want to take this a step further, the Kolbe A Index or the Color Code Personality Test are great resources that evaluate your unique talents and abilities.

In my opinion, it is so hard for people to identify their talents because all students are taught the same way in our society. A quote commonly attributed to Albert Einstein says "Everybody is a genius. But if you judge a fish by its ability to climb a tree, it will live its whole life believing that it is stupid." If we constantly judge people by their lack of ability to do what we want them to do, and it's not aligned with their unique talents, what do you think that's going to do to their mental health? It could keep them from fulfilling their purpose in life. Unfortunately, that's how our entire education system works.

I know for a fact that there are foster children who cannot sit still at a desk for eight hours. Asking them to do so is literally torture and abuse. Their minds can't handle it, yet they are routinely forced into that uncomfortable situation. Some of them act out, and others shut down because they physically can't meet that expectation. Maybe their talent isn't listening to lectures and regurgitating facts, but it could be using their hands to create art or music. The Kind Foundation helps children in foster care identify what they're passionate about and their unique talents. Now it's time to find yours. Take some time to respond to the following questions in quadrant two.

Questions to consider

- What are your unique talents?
- What abilities do you have that come easily to you?
- Are your talents concentrated in one area, or are they diverse?
- What are your physical gifts?
- What are your spiritual gifts?
- Do any kinds of relationships come easy to you?
- Are you gifted in your career or business?

Quadrant 3: Values

Values are chosen. This quadrant refers to the rule book you have written for your own life. The challenge people typically face here is that their value systems make it impossible to actually experience the full expression of their gifts, talents, and strengths. Many people have essentially blocked their own passions because they are driven by a conflicting set of values.

Values are like labels. We put labels on ourselves, and other people put them on us.

Values can be the way in which you act, such as with respect and gratitude, or maybe you put a lot of value on life, relationships, and connections. Any of those may be important to you now, but maybe you were raised in a home where your family valued safety, security, and minding your own business. A lot of people develop values later in life that conflict with how they were raised. That internal strife means your worldview does not match your self-view.

As you begin the process of creating a new value set, you need to explore your current values, your childhood values, and where they all came from. Be specific when you write these down. Think about why they matter to you.

Questions to consider:

- What do you value in life?
- Do you value family time?
- Do you value physical fitness?
- Do you value generosity?
- What values do you innately hold dear?
- Who "passed" your values down to you? Parents, friends, mentors?
- Where did they come from?
- Are your values labels that people have placed on you? Do you think you display them?

Quadrant 4: Beliefs

There are certain roles and responsibilities that you and I act out in our lives. It doesn't matter what your current situation may be (i.e. you're married, you're single, you have kids, your dogs are your kids, you own a business, etc.), the roles you play on a daily basis are crucial in the expression of your beliefs. These may be your religious beliefs, but they can also be about anything. Your beliefs limit or accelerate your ability to fully express your gifts, talents, and strengths. For example, I believe in fairness and equality. I believe in the rule of law and that no one is above it. I believe in justice. I do not sit idly by or ignore bullies. I detest them! They make me sick to my stomach, every form of them. I am a protector…I am a sheepdog!

That is a core belief that I hold dear. It's part of who I am—not just an idea. My anti- bullying beliefs, along with several others that I hold sovereign, have shaped my life. They have molded me into who I am. They have helped me to stay focused on children in foster care who have been abused, neglected, and who don't believe they have any value, or that there is even anyone in their corner.

Questions to consider:

- What do you believe to be true for yourself and the world around you?
- Have you developed your own beliefs, or were they given to you by someone else?
- Where do you draw a line in the sand?
- What do you stand for?

The center of your blueprint

Now that you've finished brainstorming, revisit all four quadrants and look over what you wrote. Were you honest with yourself? For example, did you list passions that are as essential to your life as oxygen? Or did you just write things that interest you? If you can't identify what you really want, and why that matters, then there is no point proceeding through the book, yet. You want to come out of this with a purpose that defines you. That will allow people to see you for who you truly are, which is a good thing. We need more authenticity in this world. More real, less fake. More you, less curated social media imagery.

If you can stand tall and declare what you want, then the world will align you with the right people with the right ideas and resources. When you realize that God has a purpose for your life, and you embrace it, nothing can stand in your way. Miraculously, where there were once people preventing you from opening doors, He replaces them with people who will open the door for you. Your mission statement is your declaration that announces to the world what you believe and what's important in your life. When you operate with a clear purpose and a sense of urgency, nothing else matters. The rest of life simply becomes noise.

When you have sorted this out, write your mission statement in the center of the blueprint. Declare this statement daily and it will become what you stand for and all that you will become in the future. Make it a clear and concise statement declaring to the world "Here is who I am. This is my mission!"

Commitment

You're going to need commitment to be successful with your mission. People are fearful of that word because they have the wrong idea about what it means. How do you react to it? The topic of commitment interests me because it evokes such strong emotion. Commitment means desiring a certain outcome and being willing to do whatever it takes to get that outcome. You'll do whatever it takes, and you embrace the hardships standing in your way. A lot of people think commitment means something permanent. Nothing in this world is permanent, though, except for change.

To be honest, I was afraid of commitment for a long time and even used it as an excuse. For example, if I tried something and failed, I could just feign that I was never committed in the first place. It wasn't the lie I would tell others that scared me, though, it was that I had to convince myself that I never actually wanted something I knew deep down mattered a lot to me.

I learned major lessons about commitment from the Wake Up Warrior program, where a lot of my breakthroughs have happened. The program helped me shift my mindset from scarcity to abundance. I learned to create a life of meaning and purpose through daily habits and behaviors. I realized that the stories inside my head about lack and scarcity are not true, no matter how loudly I heard them. In fact, stories of abundance are more likely to be true, and true prosperity is actually rather simple to achieve. That doesn't mean it is easy, though. I will never tell you that commitment is easy, but I will tell you that it's worth it. When you follow this simple formula, you become laser-focused on your purpose. If you commit to the process, the results will astonish you.

Before people commit, they often want to be 100% certain that what they are doing will work, and that they will get the results they want. This is true when people search for workout programs, relationships, jobs, churches, etc. That's not how God works, though, when it comes to commitment. He wants you to take the first step and promises to meet you half way.

Committing first drives your courage. The more actions you take toward that commitment, the more courage you feel. That drives clarity. Your eyes are shown another piece of the puzzle every time you take a courageous step.

My wife and I lost our first child about 10 years before I started writing this book. Financially, we were not making ends meet and were about to lose our home. We reluctantly dipped our toes into the world of foster care, and we discovered it was our purpose. We found hope in our hopeless situation through committing ourselves to helping children in the foster care and adoption community heal from life's hurts. Now we fund our purpose through our private foundation and use a family trust to grow our wealth. We tackle every day with that purpose. It drives our energy, creativity, and our passion as a family. Today, our lives are completely unrecognizable from 10 years ago. This reminds me of a quote from the famous life coach Tony Robbins: "Most people overestimate what they can do in a year, and they dramatically underestimate what can be done in 10 years."

After we discovered our mission, I still had hard work to do on myself. I told myself so many lies about what I was entitled to as a business owner and family man. I was stretched thin trying to provide for my family and run two businesses. When business was not doing well, I felt shame and guilt. My pattern became turning those emotions outward onto my family. I had pictures in my mind of how "things should be." If I didn't get what I wanted at home I became loud and aggressive. I'll be the first to admit that I can be scary when I'm angry.

One evening, I came home after a rough day at work to find my wife and oldest daughter anticipating my arrival by scrambling to clean the kitchen as fast as possible. When I opened the door, I heard my seven-year-old say "dad's home." My wife asked her "what kind of mood is he in?" My daughter said she would go check, and when she came running around the corner, I was crushed. They had no idea I overheard what they were saying, and it devastated me that they had to worry about my mood.

Instead of connecting with my wife about my shame and guilt from work, I got into the negative pattern of lashing out at her. My mentor says that "hurt people hurt people," and that was me. I had to break the pattern and come to grips with the conclusion that my pain had nothing to do with anyone else but me. Once we own the bad emotions, we can fix them. As married men and business owners, we can't even get to that point with a scarcity mindset. Your patterns need to be interrupted. Someone, or something, needs to wake you up. Instead of sedating and isolating myself, I had to shatter those beliefs, lean in, and learn how to connect with my family again. I had to learn how to be the dad who showed up every day with acts of kindness and love notes for my girls. We have to act in intentional and significant ways to improve relationships that matter. I committed to writing notes of affection and affirmation to my daughters and sending my wife a video that uses those two words every day.

Your money, finances, and taxes are no different. Interrupt those patterns, shift your mindset, and level up your skill set in those areas so that you can play a different game. Living a mission-driven lifestyle, and creating an environment where that is at the core of your family, will shift your perspective on everything. Simple tasks will become new opportunities to create more philanthropic capital. Boring meetings with executives will become opportunities to talk about the great work your foundation has done. It helps strengthen bonds and create relationships that otherwise might not exist. Doors will open and conversations that you never would have had will start to happen. The key to achieving that outcome, however, is commitment. It is worthy to repeat that commitment is something that is simple, but it's not easy.

Wake Up Warrior teaches men that life is all about the patterns and habits that form your days, weeks, months, years, and decades. In order to change your habits, you've got to commit to doing something different. We all understand this at a surface level. In order to make a physical change, such as getting your body into shape, you have to make several commitments in different areas of your life. If you buy a gym membership, that's a financial commitment. You also commit your time, energy, and effort when you work out and eat right. All of these commitments become part of your daily routines, patterns, and habits.

You have to be committed if you want to shift your mindset. You must become a person who is actually capable of pulling that off and staying committed. The new you must be remolded and reshaped in order to pull off the vision you have for your future. You must be willing to commit at the highest possible level. This will ensure that you not only understand the structure and rules of the game, but that you are clear about your long-term mission and purpose. If you make this commitment, you can pass the wisdom and education down from generation to generation, just like the wealthiest families in our country have been doing for generations.

Does that scare you? Most people in our society understand very little about commitment. True commitment is evident across the four pillars of life: body, being, balance, and business. If you neglect your health it will impact other areas of your life, such as your family, business, and legacy. If you want a healthy, happy, stress-free life, and you want to wake up energized every day, you must commit to your mission and purpose on every level.

The Four B's:

- **Body**: Your physical fitness and health.
- **Being**: Your spiritual connection to your purpose.
- **Balance**: Your relationships with loved ones who add massive joy to your life.
- **Business**: Your ability to keep and grow wealth.

Committing to something bigger than yourself does something magical. It creates motion, which creates emotion and passion. The problem is that the human brain has been developing for more than 20 million years to do two things really well: conserve energy and protect us.

Essentially, any time we are forced to make a decision, no matter how big or small, our brain immediately scans for threats. Once our brain perceives a threat, we start believing the stories that we tell ourselves (both good and bad) about why something can or cannot be done. We are essentially trying to confirm what we already believe, a phenomenon known as confirmation bias.

That 20-million-year-old software program in your brain is called the sympathetic nervous system, or "lizard brain." The only way to overcome it is to step back, breathe deeply, and try to relax. The goal is to engage the frontal lobe, which is the part of the brain responsible for higher-order thought processes, communication, connection, creativity, and more. The lizard brain is responsible for protection from threats. That is why you must be willing to commit first and gain clarity later. We are often slaves to our own thought patterns when we react to stressors, or outside influences, because we want 100% clarity and certainty before we commit to anything. Unfortunately, as we learned, it doesn't work that way.

Nothing great ever happened to you when you were 100% certain and clear about what you were doing, where you were going, or what landmines you had to avoid. First, you must commit to the process of moving forward. Once you take the first step, you will gain more confidence in yourself and the process you are undertaking. As you move forward, you will see what is unfolding more clearly, and then things will make more sense. Once you see enough of the big picture, and implement certain changes, you will become more certain about your commitment.

The financial journey in this book is no different. At first, you will not understand everything about how to keep your money or grow your wealth, but you must commit first in order to live a mission-driven life. Courage, clarity, and certainty will follow. It's never the other way around, so ask yourself what you want, why it matters to you, and what you're committed to doing about it.

If this makes you nervous, good! It should! When your vision becomes bigger than your world is today, it will take massive action and commitment. It's normal to feel scared, but congratulations on having the courage to accept the challenge. In order to grow into the person who can pull off your mission, it will require change. Nothing will change until you commit to doing what is necessary to get the result you want.

Most people who have not taken the time to ask themselves the difficult "why" questions tend to be noncommittal. Unfortunately, this has become the norm, and I would estimate that 99% of people in our society are not committed to a cause. They are afraid of commitment, which causes them to drift, not focus on anything meaningful, and just live day to day.

You have bigger plans, though. You've spent your whole life building and growing in order to give back and make a difference. Don't stop now. Revisiting your mission statement is the most important habit you can form every day. When you become mission-driven, you will wake up on fire, serve at the highest level possible, connect with people at their heart level, and spread an infectious amount of love and joy. That is what makes life great. Whoever you believe yourself to be, whoever you know in your heart that you are, that's who will drive everything that you do on a daily basis. Being clear about who you are and what you're about is the most important thing you could ever do. Along your journey, you will begin to awaken, activate and apply all of these principles.

"The biggest risk is not taking any risk. In a world that is changing really quickly, the only strategy that is guaranteed to fail is not taking risks."

- Mark Zuckerberg

CHAPTER SIX

THE HISTORY OF ECONOMIC COLLAPSE: YOU'RE NOT PREPARED FOR THIS—SIT DOWN

I've learned some tough lessons over the years, but it's all worth it when I get to teach clients how to avoid similar mistakes and protect their wealth. In 2001, when we sold mall.com to a venture capital firm for a big profit, we decided our next move should be to roll the wealth we generated from the sale into a second company with an even bigger idea. Operating under the assumption that the dot-com craze would never end, we all expected a 10x return.

Unfortunately, we were very, very wrong.

During the height of the dot-com era, we were spending millions on company trips, perks for employees, and marketing deals. In 1999, we even spent $4 million to become the title sponsor for the Mall.com 500 IndyCar Series race at the Dallas Motor Speedway. When the dot-com bubble burst, we called our investors to ask for another round of funding for our new concept. They didn't just say "no," but *"hell no."* Overnight, the world to which we had grown accustomed came crashing down around us. As I write this book almost 20 years after that bubble burst, the brevity of our financial memory in the country amazes me.

I decided to take a break from the internet industry and "semi-retired." During this time, I noticed a lot of the friends I had previously worked with at Dell were retiring early (before the crash) and purchasing real estate. It seemed to me that this was the next "big thing," so I began to study the markets and learn how to play this new game.

A year later, I felt I had learned enough about the market, so I started in real estate lending and investing. By 2005, I had made a bunch of money and was fortunate enough to have soaked up an immense amount of knowledge about the global markets. While my firm continued to be successful, one thing continued to bother me. The enthusiasm around buying and selling made the industry's psychology feel eerily similar to the craze of the dot-com era. The "it's- never-going-to-end" feeling was way too familiar.

Later in 2005, it became clear to Kyle Bass, a trusted friend from my diving days, that the "crowd" was ignoring several market warning signals. Jobs and incomes are the two biggest economic indicators of real estate, and they were both declining while real estate values continued to climb at a staggering rate. That December, Kyle used $34 million of his own money to start his own hedge fund, Hayman Capital Management. Previously, he worked at Legg Mason and had also been the youngest fund manager at Bear Sterns. Based on the warning signs, he feared mortgage-backed securities were in dire trouble. He theorized that if people were unable to pay their increasing mortgages on homes that were rapidly growing in value, those mortgage-backed securities would default. He took his theory a step further, raised $107 million in capital, and used those funds to bet against MBS. Over the next 18 months, he watched his hedge fund grow more than 800%. Now, he is an icon in the hedge fund world and is considered to be one of the brightest financial minds of our time.

Unfortunately for me, I was part of the crowd ignoring the warnings. I never believed Kyle when we discussed his predictions. Of all the mistakes I have made, the ones I made while following the herd hurt the most. When I take advice from guys like Kyle, and stay away from what everyone else is doing, I tend to see opportunities. He is a master of researching the markets and discovering that type of opportunity.

As Kyle's hedge fund was exploding, I joined a renowned group of industry experts as a founding member of The National Institute of Financial Education. The NIFE consisted of like- minded financial services professionals who were trying to alert people to the growing problems in the housing markets. Our goal was to show people how wealth cycles of asset classes worked. We educated people about how to preserve and protect their wealth before it was unknowingly and unnecessarily transferred into another asset class.

As the wealth in real estate grew, and incomes and jobs declined, problems became worse for homeowners as well as the banks that held the MBS. Those who understood the problem were savvy enough to liquidate and move their wealth into the next asset class that was undervalued at the time. Those who refused to learn the lessons of wealth cycles and wealth transfer were the ones who suffered most. In 2008, similar to 2001 with dot-com stocks, we witnessed the transfer of wealth from real estate assets to another asset class. The real estate bubble officially began to collapse.

It was 1:45 a.m. on Sept. 15, 2008, when Lehman Brothers Bank filed for Chapter 11 bankruptcy protection after the massive exodus of most of its clients, drastic losses in its stock, and the devaluation of its assets by credit agencies. It was the largest bankruptcy in U.S. history and was a major domino in the global financial crisis. Kyle's predictions came true, and companies, investors, and families lost fortunes.

The most painful part is that this all could have been avoided had people understood the consistent theme that surrounds every economic collapse. Here is how that cycle develops:

- The rich get richer, and the poor get poorer. The world's 100 richest people became $241 billion richer in 2012.

- The middle class gets squeezed out.

- Wealth cycles of asset classes (bubbles and collapses) become the norm. In 2012, $154 billion was pulled out of the markets.

Currently, the Federal Reserve is in a crisis that is 10 times worse than it was in 2008. None of the behavior has changed, and the problems that existed in MBS have not gone away. Problems with the banks didn't go away when they were rescued, either, they just shifted balance sheets. Now everything exists on the Federal Reserve's balance sheet, as well as the balance sheets of central banks around the world.

Where did all that wealth go?

The scary part is that 99.9% of the crowd got the crisis wrong. The top .1%, the ultra- wealthy, understood this (or paid millions to money managers who understood this).

In 2010, the median net worth in the U.S. hit its lowest point since 1969. The net worth of many Americans fell by nearly 40% between 2007 and 2010. A large part of this was due to the collapse in the housing market.

We are currently experiencing the largest wealth transfer in the history of mankind. It's important to understand that the problems of the housing crisis did *not* go away. The problems simply transferred from the private balance sheets of banks onto federal (or sovereign) balance sheets in countries around the world.

Here is your call to action. If you understand this, you will be able to preserve and protect what you've built. You will also have the opportunity to profit from this wealth transfer. This is an opportunity only afforded to us once in 100 years. If you don't understand this, keep reading!

In order to truly comprehend what is going on, you must look at the history of monetary policy. At the end of World War I, the world replaced laissez-faire with political motivation in economic and monetary affairs. Basically, governments and central planners began to shift economic affairs away from wealth creation and into wealth destruction. This is what motivated British economist John Maynard Keynes to write that he looked forward to the "euthanasia of the rentier" (a term for saver that he used to convey disdain) in the concluding notes to his book *The General Theory of Employment, Interest and Money*. He wanted the rentier to be replaced by "communal saving through the agency of the State to be maintained at a level which will allow the growth of capital up to the point where it *ceases to be scarce.*" Monetarists in charge of central banks joined Keynes in this objective, acting as the agency by which savings are destroyed and capital is made to be scarce no longer.

Alasdair Macleod, head of research at The Goldmoney Holding in England, summed up the situation by saying "Unfortunately for us, Keynes won the intellectual argument, and we have been paying the price ever since." What you are seeing today is the same pattern repeating itself. The wealth cycles of asset classes are shifting once more. It's the Panic of 2008, but it's happening on a much larger scale. Instead of real estate as the asset class, it's fiat currencies around the world that are in jeopardy of collapsing. Many countries are currently experiencing their own Great Depressions. Trade wars are heating up, currency wars are taking place, and another world war is next.

Our entire financial system is based on credit expansion instead of labor and productivity. Our Founding Fathers were against the idea of a central bank because they feared it would give the federal government too much control. However, in 1791, Secretary of the Treasury Alexander Hamilton, established the First Bank of the United States to loan money to foreign countries, such as Great Britain, that needed cash infusions. That first central bank operated until its charter expired in 1811, and the Second Bank of the United States was founded five years later.

President Andrew Jackson, who took office in 1829, thought a central bank symbolized how a privileged class could oppress the will of common Americans. Jackson won that political fight in 1833 and redistributed funds to various state banks in a move to "empower the common man." The pendulum swung back the other way with the creation of the Federal Reserve in 1912, though, and we have had a debt-driven financial system ever since.

You know that feeling you get in your bones when something is just not right? I feel it, and I know you can, too. In reality, the only reason the world economy is teetering along is because the central banks continue to print money. The problem is, that by printing money, they are actually devaluing and debasing the currencies.

Why would anyone *want* to hold onto fiat money? Think about this: there is more than $800 trillion in derivatives (paper assets) worldwide, versus $64 trillion in real asset value. In many of these situations, the quantitative analysis is already done. It's just a question of when and how this will unravel. I think it's important to pay attention to the fact that in the last 10 years, debt around the world (this is total credit market debts, debts on balance sheets, sovereign obligations, corporate debts, and household debts) has grown from $80 trillion to just over $200 trillion. We are witnessing the world's largest peacetime accumulation of debt in history. You know how this ends, right? In war.

I don't know which countries will be involved, but I am certain that in the next few years, you will see wars erupt—and not just small ones. You will see more social unrest, as well. We saw huge riots in Greece during its economic collapse, and you are going to see huge riots in other parts of the world over food (or the lack of food) that are derivatives of the financial problems we are seeing. The reality is that we are exporting inflation to other nations, and moving forward it is going to be a major problem. Think about this: if all of the world's 7.8 billion people consumed as much as the average American, it would require the resources of more than five planet Earths to sustainably support everyone.

A lot of the social unrest going on in our world is tied to these dramatic food-price increases. In short, the biggest driver of the price of food is the price of oil. Therefore, as we hit peak oil, are we also hitting peak food? The price of bailing out credit junkies in the rich world is driving up the price of survival in the poor world. In a world where billions of people want what you have (and might be prepared to do anything politically, militarily, or financially to achieve this), how will it end? Nobody is going to announce that a collapse is coming. You're going to have to recognize it for yourself.

During the Tequila Crisis of 1994, the Mexican government affirmed almost daily that it would not default or devalue. One day after officials said "we won't devalue," they devalued by 60%. The government is never going to tell you, but it is going to happen.

There are several well-documented cycles of fiat currencies throughout history. The Roman denarius, for example, was made from pure silver during prosperity and dropped down to 0.02% silver at the collapse of the Roman Empire. In 1525, Renaissance-era mathematician Nicolaus Copernicus said "nations are not ruined by one act of violence, but gradually and in almost imperceptible manner by the depreciation of their circulating currency, through excessive quantity."

In the 1930s, France inflated the franc so much over a 12-year period that it lost 99% of its value and other countries no long accepted it for trade.

More recently in 1999, Argentina went through an economic collapse and restructuring.

Two of the key factors in its currency collapse were increased debt due to out-of-control spending and large amounts of borrowed money by former Argentine President Carlos Menem. Within one year of hitting the 50% debt-to-GDP ratio, Argentina defaulted on all debt, riots broke out, and political turmoil ensued.

The examples don't stop there. The U.S. dollar has lost 96% of its purchasing power (original value) since inception. Our country's debt-to-GDP ratio is more than 130%, and we are currently borrowing money at an unprecedented rate. In the 10 years preceding this book's release, external debt has grown from $6 trillion to $28 trillion, while tax revenues declined due to job loss and retirees leaving the workforce.

British economist and author Sir Josiah Stamp said it best back in 1927. "If you wish to remain the slaves of the bankers and pay the cost of your own slavery, let them continue to create money and control the nation's credit."

In the near future, the plug is going to be pulled, and no one is going to lend anyone any more money. We saw this on a small scale in

2008, when credit markets around the world froze. There was so much risk that banks not only refused to lend money to individuals and businesses, they refused to even lend money to each other. Around the world, central banks, such as the U.S. Federal Reserve, calmed financial markets by pumping out trillions of dollars in emergency lending. This gave many the perception that things were returning to normal, but as Kyle Bass consistently points out: "we are in anything but a normal situation."

The take away? Debt has skyrocketed, and we're not going to pay it back—ever. Our creditors will eventually resort to mafia tactics and "break some legs" when the debt is not paid. I don't mean to make these debts seem trivial. These aren't gambling debts, they are debts of entire sovereign nations. The tools used to "take care of it" won't be crowbars or baseball bats, but rather soldiers, tanks, and intercontinental ballistic missiles.

The reality is that war is coming—just as it has throughout history—and the 99% of Americans who believe in a benevolent, all-knowing, and caring government will be the last ones to get the memo. You can choose to ignore the warning signs at your own peril. Central banks are beginning to not trust each other, and global "Kumbaya" and handholding is coming to an end. Just look at Germany: it is repatriating its gold from the U.S. Federal Reserve. Forty-five percent is initially going to be moved, but this likely will take place much sooner than the initial timeframe.

Central planners are trying with all their might to force people into behaviors and financial assets (vis-à-vis the stock and bonds markets) that are in direct contrast to their logic or long-term financial well-being. This is the height of immorality, not to mention hubris. There is a 0% chance of any Fed exit—ever. This entire experiment ends with civil unrest and martial law. That is the exit strategy.

Let's face it: the current model of saving for retirement and investing in paper stocks, bonds, and paper assets is not working. For more than 70 years, we have blindly followed Wall Street executives and economists without questioning their ideas—only to discover that they were wrong.

As the fiat currencies around the world continue to devalue and collapse, all assets that are denominated in those currencies will become worthless! The way to avoid falling victim to the impending currency collapse is to understand the practices of the ultra-wealthy. Why?

Because they are using tools that allow them to preserve their wealth so they can continue to follow the wealth cycles of asset classes and grow their wealth from generation to generation.

The wealthy mindset is comprised of four core principles:

1. They stop the bleeding and keep what they make—always!

2. They do not follow the herd. They use methods such as banking to grow wealth and earn uninterrupted compounding. They don't risk their wealth in the market.

3. They understand that if you are not constantly protecting and growing wealth, then you are losing wealth. Consistent, uninterrupted compounding is key, not the volatility you see in the market.

4. Ownership, or title, follows taxes and liability. This means that they give up ownership, but never lose control of their assets and wealth.

The wealthy mindset

When we really examine the ultra-wealthy (the top .1%), historically, one theme becomes crystal clear: *Wealthy people think differently.* It's what we refer to as the *wealthy mindset*. The wealthy don't think in terms of "absolute dollars" because they know that is made up of manipulated currency. "Absolute dollars" is a term they use to keep score. Their true wealth is found in the value of assets they own, as well as the purchasing power of those assets. This is a crucial concept to understand because it is why you might believe things are "getting too expensive," and why you might be worried about not having enough.

Let's take a closer look. Typically, diversified portfolios are stocks, commodity stocks, real estate stocks, bonds, etc. They are all paper assets, which are traded on the exchanges. For 70 years, the herd has invested in IRAs, 401(k) plans, and mutual funds without questioning how the markets work or how wealth in those paper assets is moved and manipulated. In fact, Wall Street has manipulated the money in such a way that it seems too difficult to get away from it.

So, where do the ultra-wealthy put their wealth? They put it in physical productive assets to create a hedge against the devaluation of currencies. For instance, the following are examples of things that outpace inflation: real physical productive assets (asset-backed lending, real-estate, oil, and gas wells), cash-flow businesses, properly structured insurance contracts, energy companies, and technology.

Notice the trend? The ultra-wealthy let their money do the work for them instead of working for their money. They diversify into physical assets that hold value and produce revenue or income. When they hedge in other physical assets that outpace inflation it protects the purchasing power of their wealth. They understand wealth cycles of asset classes and follow them from undervalued to their peak, which is when they transfer their wealth into other asset classes that are undervalued. When the crowd is running into an asset class, the ultra-wealthy are typically running out of it. They do *not* follow the advice of the "licensed professionals" on Wall Street.

Here are some startling statistics that are commonly thrown around in the financial services industry:

Out of 100 people over the age of 75,

1. 74 are dead.

2. 21 are on government aid.

3. 4 are barely surviving.

4. Only 1 is thriving.

The wealthy mindset helps these individuals consistently grow their wealth from generation to generation without risk. They will never have their wealth dry up or have to work at age 70, 80, or 90. The richest .1% increased their wealth by more than 100% in the past 20 years. In fact, this group's wealth actually accelerated during the financial crisis. Due to technological advances in medicine and lifestyle, we all are living longer, healthier lives. Actuarial tables tell us a newborn baby girl is expected to live an average of 135 years! So, keeping those statistics in mind, if you retire at 65, how will you outlast your retirement income? How will Social Security, Medicare, Medicaid, etc., survive in the future?

We need to ensure that as many people as possible will be able to not just survive this crisis and prepare for retirement, but actually *thrive*

> "A PRUDENT MAN FORESEES THE DIFFICULTIES AHEAD AND PREPARES FOR THEM; THE SIMPLETON GOES BLINDLY ON AND SUFFERS THE CONSEQUENCES."
> – PROVERBS 22:3

in this new economy. We understand we cannot save everyone, but the more people we can save, the better off we will be as a nation. We will also be more prepared as leaders to help our families, friends, and loved ones.

I truly believe that before this collapse happens, it is critical for all of us to understand these concepts, ideas, and strategies—not just so we and our families can prosper, but so we can help our communities. Why? Because the bottom line is we will need to help those who have nothing when they are completely wiped out financially. It will be up to us to help those who are less fortunate—that is the mission!

What is everyone searching for? What are people grasping for right now? Control. Control of their future, their wealth, and their family's decisions. I am writing this to empower you to clearly see the problems, evaluate your current position, and educate you on a roadmap.

"Why do I need succession planning? I'm very alert, I'm very vibrant. I have no intention to retire."

- Sheldon Adelson,
founder of Las Vegas Sands Corporation.

CHAPTER SEVEN
EXPOSING THE GAP

M atthew Chapter 7 teaches that if you build a foundation on sand, nothing will last, but if you build on rock, you can create a life as big as you want. Business owners must figure out how to stop the bleeding if they want to build a rock-solid foundation. I'm going to walk you through three steps that will help you keep the money you've been paying in taxes and protect your family's legacy. People ask me all the time why these strategies have been so elusive and difficult. Why is living a purpose-driven life in the 1041 system the exception rather than the norm? To get to the bottom of those questions, you need to understand the systemic and purposeful issues that are working against you.

Every day across our country, hard-working business owners, entrepreneurs, and investors are losing the money they worked for without even realizing it. While you sleep, you're losing money. While you eat, you're losing your legacy to taxes, lawsuits, creditors, etc.

Business owners live in constant worry about keeping and growing their money. Most people don't even dream about creating a legacy that will last for generations because they don't realize it's an option. Only the wealthy have known about this option, but soon you will, too.

Since the creation of the Federal Reserve Bank, and the expansion of credit, our nation has evolved to forget what it was like to produce value, grow wealth, and live in abundance. No matter how successful business owners become, they operate with a scarcity mindset. They may be great at producing wealth, but they can't keep their money. Or, they're great at keeping money, but they can't grow it. How have we lost these simple principles?

The three steps I'm going describe in this chapter represent a huge part of the process I work through with my clients. If you're still not sure about trading in your clunky, older-model 1040 tax return lifestyle for the more efficient 1041 system, these steps will show you how much that decision could cost you. This allows us to break the information down to show the effect of their potential savings in a detailed analysis.

One of the first things my team does for a client is use the tax returns and other financial records they provide us to create a side-by-side comparison, or business cash flow and tax strategy evaluation, which shows their current taxable liability. To show you what I mean, I want to walk you through an example client, who I'll refer to as Steve. Steve is 42, owns a successful medical practice, and makes about $450,000 a year. We calculate what he pays in taxes and show him what would happen if we put it in life insurance policies, which traditionally have earned dividends of anywhere from 4-15% based on what rates are doing. We'll use 6% for this example, which is what Steve actually received last year in dividends. If Steve did this every year until he retired at 65, his income potential would be more than $14.5 million. His wealth potential would be almost $30 million if he were able to save it all. Right now, though, he is paying taxes at a 30% rate. If he kept that up, by the time he turns 65, it would add up to $8.7 million gone and lost forever! If he became one of my clients, he would potentially get to keep and use that amount by the time he retired. Now, what if he lives to be 95? If we use the same numbers, it comes out to more than $81 million in tax savings. When you put that into a properly structured financial contract, such as life insurance, it earns uninterrupted dividends, becomes your "trust vault," and has the potential to explode in value.

Now that Steve knows what it might cost him to keep using the 1040 tax return, we need to figure out how we get him from where he is today to where he wants to be with that $81 million in his pocket growing and compounding consistently. To do that, we use these three steps:

Step 1: Clarify where you are

People generally resist focusing on the facts of their current situation because they want their lives to be driven by fiction. Normally, my clients talk about what they did in the past and where they are headed, but rarely have I found someone who is rooted in today. People constantly bounce from what they did to what they want to do. This never allows you to focus on what you must do today in order to become the person who can pull off this amazing game.

Creating a Gap Map exposes the gap between today's facts and the possibilities for your future. As you go through this step, I encourage you to think beyond your financial life. Get clear on every aspect of your life and the costs associated with your current reality. Are you truly living out your purpose and the life you were intended to live? If you're not, you must ask yourself what you truly want and why that matters to you. Again, I'm not just talking about money. There are costs to your body, spirit, relationships, family life, etc.

I ask clients to provide tax returns from the last couple of years and fill out as much information as possible. It shows commitment when clients send personal information to someone they don't know that well, and it shows me that they cleared a major psychological hurdle. Next, I have clients put together a Gap Map so we can analyze everything. Finally, we meet to expose the gap between where they are today and where they want to be. The gap doesn't just exist financially. We outline everything that has to do with the 4 B's: body, being, balance, and business.

The reason we don't just focus on money is because we know that how you do one thing is how you do everything. How you treat your body is how you're going to treat your business and manage your trusts and foundations. People have to get in the right mindset. If you're not taking care of your body, your temple, how are you going to be as a steward of your trust and foundation? The tax code is all about your intent. If your intent isn't pure, you will find yourself in trouble. The same might be said about your intent when it comes to other areas in your life.

You have to live a different life if you want to make that shift. The same thing is true for your being. If you are disconnected from God, and living a life without purpose, you have to make that shift. We ask clients to give us the facts about these areas of their lives, but we stay away from how they feel about it at first. There is great power in feelings and emotion. We must be able to focus those feelings in order to produce the fruit we want. The formula we follow is facts, feelings, focus, and fruit. We have to get the facts first, and then we link them to feelings during our one-on-one sessions. Those feelings will drive your focus, which ultimately produces your fruit. If you're not satisfied with the fruit you have produced, you have to go backward and start looking at the facts again and ask yourself how you feel about them. None of that will be possible if you're lying to yourself and others about the facts of where you are today.

Step 2: Create a roadmap with measurable targets

Once we're clear about the present and the cost of continuing on the same path, we can shift our attention to the future. What we measure, we act on. What we don't measure falls by the wayside and never gets done. If you set a target to lose weight, you have to get on a scale to track your progress. Otherwise, you can't be sure if your daily actions are working, or if you need to correct your course. If a captain of a ship sails just one degree off his path, he will reach a totally different destination. Setting meaningful and specific targets can help you stay on track. If you don't set these targets, you will wander in the dark. Remember, how you do one thing is how you do everything. If you can fix the broken system you're currently in, you have a chance at making major moves for your business and family. Always remember that the difference between standing water and boiling water is just 1°. The difference between living a purpose-driven lifestyle, and never fulfilling your purpose on earth, could be the difference between the 1040 and 1041—just one number. Think about that.

Life is a game of expansion. If you grow in each of the four areas that we set targets in, you will not recognize yourself in a year. I get passionate when I'm discussing finances with a client and our conversation shifts to being about their worldview and self-view. The goal of shifting is to have breakthroughs, and I literally view myself as being in the business of breakthroughs, not finance.

Be honest with yourself when you answer the questions I have for you below. Imagine what your ideal life would look like in the four quadrants.

Use these steps as a guide to create your roadmap:

- Commit to making one change in each of these areas: body, being, balance, business.

- Write how your life would ideally look in 12 months if you stayed committed.

- Once you have described what your life would look like, break the year down into four 90-day challenges. These will make changes that seem impossible feel more manageable and allow you to correct your course more frequently.

- Break the quarterly challenges into monthly milestones, then weekly targets. Once you're able to review progress weekly, you can set new action strategies for the following week, as necessary.

- Each week, set aside 20-60 minutes to reflect on how the past week went for you in all four areas of your life. Rate yourself 1-10 in each category. Write down what worked and what didn't.

- If something is working, then continue on that path. If not, think about the cost of not being at your best and the impact that has on the other areas of your life.

- After reflecting, write down one thing that must happen in the next week in order for you to meet your 90-day challenge. I call this your "door." Just focus on one area (mine is usually business) and set a measurable target.

- Now decide what four "keys," or supporting steps, need to be accomplished to open your door for the week. For example, if your door is to post a marketing video on YouTube, your four keys may look like this:

    o Setup a YouTube channel
    o Write the script.
    o Record the video.
    o Edit the video.

When you break down your 90-day challenges into weekly goals and their supporting tasks, you are able to collapse time and focus all of your energy, money, and emotion on your mission and purpose. You will hit your targets so much faster than you ever thought possible if you develop this pattern. This game is all about consistency and course correction along the way.

Step 3: Get accountable

Scheduling a monthly check-in call with a mentor, coach, or trusted friend, is a great way to maintain your progress. I hold them with my clients every month. Whoever you meet with, you should be able to clearly communicate what target you focused on, your progress, and your next steps. The important principle here is consistently meeting with people who have similar goals and interests. This will help you create more power and certainty in your life. Keep the conversations you have with your accountability partner focused. Catch them up on your progress over the last month, update them on where you stand today, and then decide what you need to talk about next month. What I care about is if clients are on or off target. If they're on target, great, they keep going. If they're off target, then we need to course correct.

Accountability is important because you currently lack the capacity to meet your target. How do I know? If you could already pull this off, you would already be doing it and wouldn't need help. The good news is that you're no different than I was when I started this journey.

Today, I have the ability to impact hundreds of children in the foster care community and make major moves with my family's wealth within our trusts and foundations. I wasn't always in the position to do this, though. I had to reach out proactively to get guidance along the way. I sought advice from mentors and other people who had already been playing this game. Having access to these people (and their teams of advisors) allowed me to learn the 1041 system myself. Sure, I had to correct my course several times, but now I'm making a bigger impact for kids who are in difficult situations.

Once you've connected with someone who can hold you accountable, schedule your meetings every month for the first year. Plan to hit milestones and celebrate those wins together along the way. During your meetings, it's perfectly fine to shift your focus in order to reach your next milestone. This transformation will not happen unless you become ruthlessly committed to your results. Details matter. If some things are not done properly, you'll never see the results you hoped for and end up frustrating yourself and your family. Much like setting a fitness target, you must have a daily action plan and make weekly course corrections along the way. The same is true for your ultimate transition to the 1041 system. It's a lifelong change, and it will ultimately change your bloodline, if you take your commitment seriously.

"In America, there are two tax systems: one for the informed and one for the uninformed. Both are legal."

- Judge Billings Learned Hand

CHAPTER EIGHT

"DON'T LET GOOD BE THE ENEMY OF GREAT."

Over the years, I have received some amazing advice from Joe Kane, a friend and mentor of mine. Joe was my boss for about six years before he retired from a major financial institution. We used to have friendly arguments about the best way to approach clients' problems within their personal economies. Joe loves everyone he meets and focuses his time, energy, money, and emotion on serving others. He is among the great giving leaders I talk about throughout this book. Joe is also a great husband, father, and leader.

He used to spend hours helping me think through possible solutions for clients, challenging me to think differently. One day, I approached him with a question about the various products and accounts we had access to at the company. Joe is a market fundamentalist, and I wanted to know why he believed in sticking with one product instead of another. He went through the whole process of asking me challenging questions about structure of products, costs going forward, and differences between two specific products I was looking into for a client. At one point, I turned to him and asked "Joe, what's the problem with clients requesting this account instead of the one you are looking at?"

"Nothing is 'wrong' with any of them," he said. "However, when you're faced with options in life, don't let good be the enemy of great!"

I thought deeply on this. "Don't let good be the enemy of great," I repeated. Wow! That one hit home hard. How often do we settle for good in our lives? We go to the gym to work out, but after a period of time, we tell ourselves "OK, that's good for today." If a colleague asks how things are going, we respond "Good, and you?" And they say "Good, thanks." We're all "good," but we're not all "great." How often have we settled for good advice instead of investing in great advice? We tend to settle for being good at giving, instead of pouring our hearts into generosity and serving. There's a cost to settling for "good" instead of investing in being "great."

This journey is no different. People who don't understand what you're doing with your wealth throughout this process will challenge you. Just look them in the eye and say "I'm not going to let good be the enemy of great. I choose great!" Choose great in all areas of your life. Be on fire to live a healthy lifestyle and to get in the best physical shape of your life. Focus on connecting with God in a way that attracts everyone around you. Be the person who everyone looks up to, a soul on fire! Create great relationships instead of settling for good enough. Those connections matter. How you show up for loved ones matters. Lastly, choose to be great at managing the resources and wealth that you've been blessed with. Don't bury your money in the ground, like in the Parable of the Talents in Matthew Chapter 25. Don't spend it frivolously, be great with it. Multiply what you've been blessed with so you can bless others. It's that simple, and it's that important not only for yourself, your family, and your future, but the world around you, as well.

If you're a business owner who wants to stop worrying about the IRS, creditors, lawsuits, and other threats to your hard-earned money, then your wait is over. I am about to reveal to you the three critical principles used by the ultra-wealthy to stop the bleeding, keep their tax dollars, and grow their wealth.

Principle #1: The two tax systems

Judge Billings Learned Hand is regarded as one of the greatest judges in our nation's history. He is one of the most widely-quoted members of the judiciary when it comes to his insight and expertise on contract, constitutional, and tax law. It probably does not come as a surprise that his quote at the beginning of the chapter is referring to the 1041 trust and foundation system versus the 1040 individual tax system.

My entire view on wealth management shifted when I began learn-ing how the ultra-wealthy keep their tax dollars and give back in more meaningful ways. What I discovered proved Judge Hand's quote to be correct. These two systems have been around since the beginning of the IRS in 1913, and both have been legal since day one.

There is a statistical anomaly commonly used by economists, but widely unknown to the average person, known as the rule of 97. It is the reason the majority of Americans use the 1040 system and have never heard of the 1041 system. The rule of 97 is a statistical represen-tation of change in the demographics and psychographics of America over 100 years of history.

According to the rule of 97, in 1897, 97% of Americans were investors, business owners, and entrepreneurs. The remaining 3% worked for them. The 97% ran businesses, created wealth, saved what they made, and reinvested it for growth. They controlled income and wealth. They produced, saved, invested into communities, and controlled their destiny. At the same time, only 3% of Americans were workers, apprentices, and "nine to fivers." This demographic changed so dramatically over the next 100 years that the numbers flip-flopped. In 1997, only 3% of Americans were business owners or entrepreneurs who created wealth, and 97% went to work for corporate America.

Why did that shift happen? Why did 97% of us work in corporate America for the other 3%? This was the result of several converging forces. When soldiers returned from the World Wars, they tended to settle down, get married, start families, and buy a small home with a white picket fence. So many people desired this, in fact, that it became the American dream. We are currently seeing a rebirth of the American dream, a renaissance of sorts, but with completely different rules. More people are leaving the workforce (by choice or by force). As more workers leave corporate America, many are becoming entrepreneurs, and we are seeing another dramatic shift unlike anything we've seen in a couple generations.

The Great Depression was another major factor that contributed to Americans leaving the farms, closing down businesses, and going to work for someone else. If you understand the principles of human behavior and economic forces, it's easy to see why people changed the way they operated when it came to money, income, savings, and debt during the depression era. Due to massive financial pressure, people avoided debt like the plague. The result was that people saved everything, presenting themselves to the world as hoarders. So many people desired stability that our economy actually went backward. Americans chose to live like servants in order to pull a paycheck and someday draw a pension. More and more people got suckered into becoming laborers in the most exceptional economy, and country, on the planet. This was why John Maynard Keynes called the American workforce "the rentier," a term meant to demean and devalue.

My wife's grandmother was a product of The Great Depression. She saved everything, including loose buttons that she collected in mason jars. "You never know when you'll need one to repair an old shirt or pair of pants," she would tell her family, who made fun of her frugality for years. They felt it would be easier to just buy another shirt at the store if a button fell off. In an ironic twist years later, the same grandchildren who laughed at her fought over her button collection when she passed away. My wife won that battle, and we still have the jars of buttons displayed in our kitchen.

America shifted from a nation of entrepreneurs to one of employees as the scarcity mindset became more prevalent. Most people gave up control of their own wealth production and began working in the factories that made up corporate America at the time. Congress took advantage of this tsunami of change through changing the 1040 tax code every chance they got in order to extract more tax dollars out of the American worker.

At the same time, word spread among the wealthy elite that the 1041 system allowed them to keep their money—unencumbered by the government. The families who began building wealth in trusts and foundations have benefitted immensely from retaining 100% of what they make. Their wealth does not leak out of their personal economies through taxes, interest expense, inflation, lawsuits, or creditors. This is how they are able to grow wealth from generation to generation. The rest of America is still beholden to operating in to 1040 system, which subjects them to taxation from every level of government. They play by the rules of the horrendous tax system largely without knowing there is a choice.

The wealthiest families from the early 1900s, such as the Kennedys and Vanderbilts, have been able to collapse time. They went from having nothing to being billionaires in two generations! That would have been nearly impossible if they had to give 50% to Uncle Sam in estate taxes alone. The Kennedys have even been able to protect their wealth and assets from ex-spouses who filed for divorce. Following a different set of rules made these family dynasties possible. Therein lies the key to success.

To better understand how two tax systems evolved, you have to go back to what the US Treasury Department requested of Congress in 1913. The Treasury Department, which basically acts as our government's accountant, went to Congress in 1913 and said the country was running low on money. The nation's wealth had been spent, yet with the growth of the West at a critical stage, we needed to invest in its infrastructure. It needed railroads, hospitals, post offices, schools, and essential government programs in order to grow.

Congress completely forgot why our forefathers started colonizing the New World in the first place. Its solution was to charge a "small" tax. Next, politicians alerted the five wealthiest families in America and told them they would be implementing a tax for only one year to help pay for the growth of our country. That seems like a reasonable request, right? Well, it turns out that these families were already unhappy with the government after the formation of the IRS earlier that year.

The IRS implemented the Internal Revenue Code, which focused on incomes and assets of the wealthy. The tax rates in the 1040 tax code were exponentially different in 1913 than they are now. Today (as of the writing of this book), our bottom bracket is 10%. The highest bracket in America right now is 37% (down from 42%), and there are five brackets in between. Back in 1913, the picture was very different: the bottom bracket was 1% for individual income earners making up to $20,000 a year. Keep in mind, $20,000 a year then is the equivalent of more than $512,000 today. The top tax bracket back in 1913 was only 7%, and it was for individual income earners who made $500,000 a year or more. That's equivalent to $13 million per year today!

Congress's request did not seem reasonable to the wealthy class in 1913. They didn't want to have any part of this new tax. They would not allow the federal government to come in and take any more of their wealth, so they came up with their own idea, to which Congress complied. The wealthy families were, after all, donors to elected officials.

The result of that idea was the 1041 system, where wealthy families could legally and ethically keep their tax dollars and grow their wealth. There was a catch, though: the wealthy elite would have to completely give up ownership of their companies, assets, and incomes. The government declared that "taxes follow title," and as such, if wealthy families insisted on owning everything personally, they would be taxed based on the new 1040 tax code. If they were to give up ownership for the good of society, have their assets held in a trust, and managed by a trustee, then they would be taxed using the 1041 tax code. Managed effectively, the trust could keep all of the tax dollars owed, if that money was "designated, distributed, or donated" by the trustee to a third party entity (per the IRC).

The rules of taxation are governed by ownership. If the owner is an individual, there are different regulations then if the owner were an entity with a unique and separate Federal Tax Identification number as well as formation of governing instruments and documents.

Principle #2: Uninterrupted compound interest

We have all heard the consistent drumbeat from Wall Street: if you invest your money in the markets consistently over a 30-year period, then it will grow into x amount of dollars at retirement due to compounding interest. Albert Einstein is commonly quoted saying "Compound interest is the eighth wonder of the world. He who understands it earns it. He who doesn't pays it." That's not an accurate quote, though, as there is a significant omission in the way people usually write it. He actually said "*uninterrupted* compound interest is the eighth wonder of the world." It's not a simple error, either, and just how significant of an omission it is will astound you. Uninterrupted compound interest is drastically different from simple compound interest. The wealthy elite all understand and live by the rule that you should never, ever, ever interrupt the compounding of your wealth.

If this is news to you, you're not alone. They don't teach this in business school, and Wall Street advisors never talk about the difference between interrupted and uninterrupted compounding. The question is, how has this principle been kept a secret? As demographics and psychographics shifted in America, and more people left their own entrepreneurial efforts in favor of working for large corporations, so did the way people kept money, grew money, and prepared for retirement.

For centuries, people created wealth and figured out how to grow it for the remainder of their lives. For our grandparents and great-grandparents, "retirement" still looked like hard work. They generated income, saved it, and reinvested it back into the business for "compounding." They did not throw retirement parties at 65 and walk away with a pension to pay their income for the rest of their lives. That posed all sorts of problems for companies with employees. At first, employees traded their time (working long hours at grueling jobs) for a modest house with a white picket fence and 2.5 children. This worked well for a while, too. A growing number of people were able to make money, save money, and improve their quality of life while working for a company. Even during the Roaring '20s, *The Great Gatsby* era, the entrepreneurs of the day created jobs for folks who, in turn, lived extraordinary lifestyles compared to the previous generation. That has always been the American dream: have more, grow more, and give more.

Uninterrupted compounding is a critical principle in every area of your life. For example, if you work out consistently, you'll notice health improvements. If you stop training, though, all the changes you noticed will fade quickly. The hard work you put in up to that point will not continue to produce results. You'll notice muscle loss, and your breathing will become more labored because you have quite literally interrupted the compounding efforts of your workouts. What is the cost of this inconsistency? It takes you further from your fitness goals and can contribute to anxiety, depression, or any number of other health issues.

The same is true spiritually. If you feel the power of meditation and prayer every morning, then it wouldn't feed your soul to quit now. Feeling an intense connection to God every day will help you focus on your mission. When you lack that consistency, it can prevent you from serving Him at the highest level. That is going to cost your legacy and future.

What about your relationships? If you commit to pouring into relationships with your spouse, children, and extended family, imagine how deep and meaningful they would become. This will look different for everyone, but an example could be committing to a weekly date night with your spouse. Benefits of those connections are clear.

The cost of inconsistency in these relationships can be painful (and expensive).

It's no different in the financial world. Wealth is not money; wealth is life, wealth is legacy. You'll leave behind more than dollars: connections, relationships, memories, information, knowledge, wisdom, etc. If this is the type of legacy you want, then you have to create it. It will not happen accidentally. I am confident about this because I understand the law of uninterrupted compounding. If you interrupt the compounding of your money, you will never be able to reach the target you set out for initially. Once again, how you do one thing is how you do everything. If you're inconsistent with your health goals, your body will not be on target. If you are inconsistent with your sense of purpose and spiritual connection, you will struggle through life and won't be able to lead others. If you interrupt the compounding of putting deposits in your relationships, your connections to your spouse and children will suffer, and loneliness and isolation will ensue.

Anything can cause an interruption to the compounding of your money. It can be a global event that rocks the marketplace, or it can simply be spending your money and liquidating an account. Any interruption of the compounding will affect your ability to grow that wealth and be able to spend that money in the future. If you have a $1 million nest egg, and you want to spend it down at $100,000 per year, or 10% per year, you can do that as long as you're consistently earning a higher rate of return than 10%. That is the model most Wall Street advisers show clients today. They feed you lines like "the market has performed $x\%$ on average, so if you want to spend your money down at $y\%$, you can because your account will average a higher return." The problems start when the market goes down and you have to spend that money. Can you dip into another pile of cash to avoid draining that account? What is your strategy for never dipping into your account, and never interrupting the compound interest, while still maintaining control and access to the money? If you were able to consistently save your tax dollars, and create an account where that money continued to earn uninterrupted compounding interest, how much wealth could you build? How much more could you do? The wealthy understand this, and they understand how to play the game of uninterrupted compounding instead of interrupted compounding.

The key to success comes down to control. Control of your money, control of the compounding, and control of how you access your wealth to buy things or to give back. You lose control when you interrupt compounding in every area of your life. If you lose control of your diet, it affects your health, stress, and anxiety level, which affects your performance everywhere. If you lose control of your ability to empathize, relationships suffer, and you're tempted to isolate and sedate yourself with alcohol or drugs. If you lose control of your sense of self or purpose, you lose connection with the source, with God, and wander aimlessly in the desert for 40 years. Maintaining control is the difference between winning and losing the game.

Einstein illustrated the power of compounding by asking if you would rather receive $1 million in one month or a penny doubled every day for 30 days. The first time I heard this, I figured it was a trick question. The doubling penny had to be the best option. I did not know how much better that option would be, though, so I took out my calculator and did the math:

Day 1: $.01
Day 2: $.02
Day 3: $.04

Day 4: $.08

Day 5: $.16

Day 6: $.32

Day 7: $.64

Day 8: $1.28

Day 9: $2.56

Day 10: $5.12

Day 11: $10.24

Day 12: $20.48

Day 13: $40.96

Day 14: $81.92

Day 15: $163.84

Day 16: $327.68

Day 17: $655.36

Day 18: $1,310.72

Day 19: $2,621.44

Day 20: $5,242.88

Day 21: $10,485.76

Day 22: $20,971.52

Day 23: $41,943.04

Day 24: $83,886.08

Day 25: $167,772.16

Day 26: $335,544.32

Day 27: $671,088.64

Day 28: $1,342,177.28

Day 29: $2,684,354.56

Day 30: $5,368,709.12

It turns out that choosing the penny option makes quite a big difference. These numbers remind me of starting a business. In the beginning, you struggle to get things going and don't turn much of a profit. If you keep at it, though, you reach the point where things take off and become easier. Starting a business is like a rocket ship taking off into space. You use 80% of your fuel during takeoff, but once it reaches a certain point, it flies smoothly with minimal fuel consumption.

Interrupting compounding is devastating to the overall growth of wealth. Instead of $5.3 million after 30 days, if you were to save the same amount of money, but interrupted its compounding by spending your savings five times during that 30 day period, you would be left with less than $2.1 million. The cost of interrupting your compounding, and spending the savings, would be more than half of your wealth in that scenario. You can use a compounding calculator to verify this for yourself.

Consider how interrupted compounding affects your wealth flow and personal economy. Leaking wealth is probably the biggest problem you don't even know you're facing. Whether it's taxes, interest, expenses, or inflation, the key to your success is plugging these holes, capturing the income, and making sure you're not leaking wealth. The wealthiest families in America use the 1041 system to stop the bleeding and capture their tax dollars upfront. They are not leaking that wealth year to year, decade to decade, or generation to generation.

If you owed $12,000 in taxes last year, and you were able to instead save it in what we call the "corpus account" (which has historically earned between 6-8% tax-free), after two decades you would have saved almost $480,000. Letting that money leak out in taxes is akin to making a $480,000 mistake. If your business is leaking more than $100,000 in taxes, that's a potential $3.9 million mistake! That's a comfortable retirement for most folks in America. If you decide to commit to one simple change, then Uncle Sam can help you retire. Imagine what impact that kind of capital could make on your family and charitable giving.

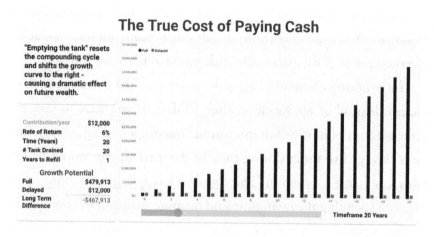

Principle #3: Give up ownership, but not control

In 1913, wealthy families who supported Congressmen and their re-election campaigns decided they weren't going to pay taxes anymore. Congress was forced to justify the extraction of taxes and the basis for such enforced extractions. That basis is known as "ownership," which is why taxes follow title, or ownership. That was a powerful idea in the minds of the ultra- wealthy. The more you own, the more you are taxed on those assets and incomes. If you made money and want to own assets, your mindset is the 1040 mindset. You believe that you are responsible for your production. Without you, there is no production.

Set your ego aside for a moment, and imagine that you are simply a steward of what you've been blessed with. If you don't own anything, the decision to move to the 1041 system is simple. The 1041 trust and foundation system lends itself to be the structure you need to live as a steward responsible for what God has blessed you with.

The beautiful thing is that if we follow these biblical principles, the rules of taxation and building wealth completely change. You begin to operate with the understanding that you are the No. 1 asset, and your business is the No. 1 investment, instead of giving up control of your wealth to some joker broker trying to find a magical ATM for you. You realize immediately that you must protect yourself and create a system of liquidity for your business. This is the revenue- generating machine that will provide for your family and legacy. The more you control the investment and growth of your business, the more you create your own ATM.

We are the only ones with the power to change the patterns and behaviors that shape our lives. We are all blessed with God-given talents and abilities; what you do with them is completely up to you. This book can open up a completely different operating system for your life and future. It's the focal point for most of the ultra-wealthy families in America, and more people are finding out about it due to information becoming easier to access. My intention is that this book (along with other titles advocating for venture philanthropy) calls attention to the painful cost of not investing your time, energy, effort, or money to understand how the financial system works. What you do with that information is totally up to you.

It shouldn't surprise you anymore that most Americans don't know about the 1041 system. This isn't just a systemic bias, it's a systemic failure. This is exactly what our Founding Fathers hated about big government. The original idea of taxation was that it would do exactly what everybody is complaining about today: tax the rich, not everyone else. The original tax rates from 1913 reflect that. Nobody paid taxes back then. Seriously! The wealthy elite who made that kind of income all participated in the 1041 system. Government was small, it did not require additional income tax to run. The entire governmental system (federal, state, and local) made up less than 5% of GDP in 1913. Today it is over 45% of GDP. In 1913, all government functions were funded with small community-based fees or revenue. From 1850 until 1913, America saw the largest economic boom and growth of real production, real GDP, in the history of the world.

Donald Trump brags that he is responsible for the greatest economic boom in our nation's history. He also calls the Obama administration an "economic disaster." That administration actually had a slightly larger economic boom, fueled by free money the government used to bail out the banks. Neither of Trump's claims hold water when you look at data and facts. The fastest- growing and most productive era with the highest percentage of wealth created was between 1850 and 1913. This was the era of little-to-no government, immense individual freedom, and hyper growth and production for all who came to America. That is what our Founding Fathers intended to happen when they signed the Constitution. Immigrants rushed to the United States, where the possibilities of attaining ownership and wealth were unlimited. They were also attracted by a government that would not get involved in their lives and did not give special treatment to certain groups of people. They did not come for free healthcare, public education, food stamps, or any of the government programs that exist now. We no longer live in the America that was founded in 1776. Our Founding Fathers did not envision anything close to the government we live under today when they established our "democratic republic."

The rule of 97 illustrates a shift in authority, power, and government. Of course, several factors were at play during this era; there was war, famine, depression, economic collapse, etc. I'm specifically talking about the transfer of power from the people to the government. This was accomplished through several pathways. The best example of transfer of power is in the transfer of wealth and ownership of assets and incomes. By definition, freedom means personal ownership. Without personal ownership, or control, of your things, you are not free. This has been true throughout the history of mankind. Slavery, as the most horrid example of this, is literally the control of another man as property.

The moment our government enacted the Internal Revenue Code, it started a slow, systemic shift resulting in loss of freedom, loss of wealth, and loss of control. At first, the tax code only affected a small fraction of American citizens. The majority of the wealthy elite chose to give up ownership of their wealth, assets, companies, and incomes in favor of the wealth- building and more advantageous 1041 tax system. Another reason so few people actually paid taxes in 1913 was because the IRS didn't begin federal tax withholding until the 1940s. Previously, it was up to the individual to decide how much and when to pay, so it's easy to see why so few people paid taxes then. Wealth continued to grow, and safety and security were the norm, not the exception. If you think about it, 1940 really wasn't that long ago. We've only seen an aggressive shift from individual rights, limited government, and abundant freedom to oppression, forced extraction of labor, taxation, and government expansion over the last 80 years. Our country has gone from individual production that was unmatched in the history of the world to abandonment of those effective principals (small government and big production).

When the government expanded, income taxes increased to fund it. The government also controls the licensing process of tax professionals. Tax attorneys, trust attorneys, and CPAs are all state licensed and limited to the statutory codes and state laws where they practice. Attorneys in Louisiana, for example, follow that state's law, which is based on French law. Texas law is based on British common law, or constitutional law. These neighboring states have completely different codes, rules, and regulations for businesses and individuals.

As the tax game took shape, the government decided they wanted to expand the federal tax code, which simultaneously and unwittingly isolated the states. State licensing boards were created to regulate industry professionals, an unconstitutional example of government expansion. Everything that is taught, trained, and drilled into tax professionals is state-specific. Since codes vary widely from state to state, most CPAs and attorneys in the financial world are never exposed to the 1041 system. They are locked into a mindset of only lowering tax brackets of the individual by hiding money in various ways, which is risky for obvious reasons. It is likely that the tax team you spend thousands of dollars to hire every year, and trust to create the best tax structure for you and your business, does not know this information.

Once you shift your mindset to a game of giving up ownership, yet maintaining control, the entire world opens up to you, your business, and your legacy. If you insist on living by the mindset of owning more stuff, then you will be taxed, and taxed, and taxed some more. I encourage you to swallow your ego, give up ownership without relinquishing control, and everything will change for you and your family for generations.

Everyone seems to be an expert about what assets you need to buy or sell these days. People will tell you that you need more real estate, land, gold, or silver. What no one considers is how that ownership will impact your income, long-term savings, tax liability, and ability to grow wealth. That game is rigged against you. Don't take shoddy advice from some CPA or attorney you met at a dinner party. They'll want you to structure an S Corporation in order to save on taxes. "You should also set up a trust," they would add. "I can get it done for you super cheap." You also don't want to give control of your wealth and assets to some joker broker who will put it in an account for you and manage it on your behalf inside a trust as the trustee. You will give up those assets forever and lose control of them. If they ever get distributed to you or future generations of your family, it will trigger a massive tax liability. Another thing financial professionals will advise you to do is set up an expensive estate plan with multiple LLCs and trusts with varying uses and abilities. None of those tactics can do what the structure of this specialized private trust, combined with a private foundation, can do.

"Anyone may arrange his affairs so that his taxes shall be as low as possible; he is not bound to choose that pattern which best pays the treasury. There is not even a patriotic duty to increase one's taxes."

- Judge Billings Learned Hand,
Helvering v. Gregory (Second Circuit)

CHAPTER NINE

CAN THIS WORK FOR ME?

"This is incredible," said Eric, a pseudonym I'll use for one of the first prospective clients who received my pitch for the 1041 system. "You're either telling the truth, or you're full of it."

That was Eric's "lizard brain" trying to do its job and protect him from disaster. It's actually a pretty common response people give me, and you may have had the same thoughts. This itch can only be scratched by asking critical questions and doing research on your part. I encourage you to fact check the 1041 system as well as any of the other information I've given you. Visit IRS.gov to find information about the 1041 document or the National Association of Enrolled Agents website (NAEA.org).

Eric was a brilliant, young internet entrepreneur from California. At 23, he was the youngest (at the time) to win the coveted Two Comma Club Award, which is given to entrepreneurs who earn more than $1 million in income from a single marketing funnel or offer. His business was set up as an LLC in California, and everything he did was in that state.

When I met him, he had just paid a retainer fee of more than $100,000 (plus costs for analysis and recommendations) to a CPA firm in San Diego. He defended this decision by saying the firm was "super expensive, so they must know everything." Three years earlier, Eric was broke and renting a tiny apartment that he could barely afford. Since then, he made $1 million in 53 days by becoming a #FunnelHacker (look it up on social media). He mastered the game of click funnels and wanted to talk to me about creating a foundation, making a bigger impact, and saving on his tax bill.

Eric wanted to consult with his high-dollar CPA firm after I described the structure, code, laws, and history behind the 1041 system. That state-licensed tax team (not a single member had a federal credential) met about his inquiry, billed him $10,000, and advised him not to move forward with the 1041 system. Instead, they tacked on another $10,000 fee for their recommendation of a statutory grantor type trust. These are only regulated and registered at the state level, which is important to note because the trust would not be protected from any government agencies at the federal level, including the IRS. In order to save on taxes, they also recommended a new captive insurance company, which would require him to give up control.

When Eric told me about their recommendations, I responded by saying "It sounds like they have a solution for you moving forward, but I have a question. Why didn't they tell you about this before?"

"Not sure," Eric replied. "I didn't think to ask that. What's the difference between what you do and what they're talking about?"

I smiled. I'm happy to be a resource for people who are exploring their financial options, but I'm not in the business of training other tax "gurus" on this stuff. I've invested hundreds of thousands of dollars and years of my life to sharpen my expertise. Then, I searched long and hard to assemble a team of the best and brightest minds to help. I could have hired the CPA firm run by my old college diving buddy. He would have done a fine job if I paid the firm a $250,000 retainer every year, up to $750 an hour for its state-licensed attorney's time, plus the $25,000-50,000 final tax prep payment. The thing is, though, just because they charge a high price doesn't guarantee that the team will understand everything.

In my experience, the wealthier the client is, the more frustrated they get when they find out about the 1041 system. They are usually in disbelief that their team hadn't already come up with this plan for them. The big five firms have elite teams who understand the 1041 system and get paid generously by their clients to do exactly what you've been learning about in this book.

Eric ended up paying $238,000 in taxes that year. What a painful number! That's a lot of capital that could have been redirected into philanthropy. It's a shame that his team couldn't keep that money in his pocket that first year—but it got worse. Business exploded, and Eric earned four more Two Comma Club Awards over the next three years. He also won the 10X Award, given to entrepreneurs who earn more than $10 million from one marketing funnel, and two more awards celebrating the $25- and $50-million milestones. Imagine how much he paid in taxes after those fiscal years. That wealth is lost forever, and he will never earn interest on any of that money.

I wasn't surprised to hear from Eric again in March of 2020. He admitted to being sick and tired of losing so much money to taxes. In fact, he was considering playing a game that several other billionaires have played and moving his residence to Puerto Rico, where you only pay 1% tax (0% for anyone up to a very high income level). I advised him that uprooting his whole life just to save on taxes was not the wisest play. He finally agreed to move forward with the 1041 structure, and now he will save millions in taxes every year for the rest of his life. His children won't even have to worry about losing money through taxes, nor his grandchildren. He will keep that money, grow his wealth, and fully fund his private foundation so he can give back in a meaningful way.

You can't be hard on yourself for not knowing or understanding this stuff. How would you have been exposed to it? The reality is that if you were not raised in one of the families who already participate in the 1041 system, you wouldn't know about it if you hadn't picked up this book.

If you had been born into one of the 200,000-plus families who participate in the 1041 system, it would simply be the way you operate on a daily basis. You would understand that you don't own anything. Your family trust owns the family assets, your business trusts owns all the business assets, and you represent your family's private foundation. As such, your lifestyle is paid for. You've probably heard of "trust fund kids." They drive around in exotic cars and say things like "it's not mine, it's owned by the family trust."

Those families are ethically keeping their tax dollars and playing by the rules, too. Paris Hilton, for example, is a trustee for the Conrad N. Hilton Foundation. She earns a modest salary for representing the family and doesn't own any of the custom, exotic cars she is known for driving. How is that possible? The better question is, how is it law-abiding? Her lawyers would argue that her lifestyle drives publicity and earns money for the foundation, which generates philanthropic capital.

The wealthy understand that the way to win the game is to "own nothing, but to control everything," like Nelson Rockefeller said. Your tax guru doesn't think this way. For my client Eric, that resulted in losing three of his top-producing years and finding this out the hard way. The lesson here is to understand who you are calling an "advisor," and to realize that you'll get different advice from federally-licensed and state-licensed financial professionals.

Systemic breakdowns

A lot of people point out systemic racism. The truth is that there are a lot of systemic breakdowns in America, and our public education system is one of the best examples. If you go to public schools, you'll be conditioned and educated to go work for someone else someday. That system has not changed in more than 100 years. It is designed by an elite few to give you skills that will benefit corporations, international conglomerates, and dynasties of the wealthiest families in America.

Many institutions of higher education were founded, or are funded, by the wealthy elite. Schools with the best funding for research opportunities attract the best faculty. They also offer more scholarship money to the brightest students. Foundations also make donations in land, buildings, artwork, and other big-tickets items. Here are some of America's wealthiest universities that received significant donations from notable foundations:

- **Harvard University:** The wealthiest university in the world. Hedge fund manager John Paulson became the largest single-gift donor in university history when he gave $400 million to the School of Engineering and Applied

Sciences. David Rockefeller and The Bill and Melinda Gates Foundation have also donated more than $100 million each.

- **The University of Texas System:** The Gates also contributed a generous amount here, along with private foundations connected to former ConocoPhillips CEO Jim Mulva and financier William Lewis Moody Jr.

- **Yale University:** In the last decade, Yale has received some of its largest single-donation contributions ever from Chinese businessman and graduate Zhang Lei, media magnate John Malone, and Franklin Resources chairman Charles Johnson.

- **Stanford University:** Stanford has been one of the leading fundraising institutions in recent history, receiving donations from the Hewlett Foundation, financiers Dorothy and Robert King, real-estate mogul John Arrillaga, and Nike co-founder Phil Knight, who gifted $400 million in 2016.

- **Princeton University:** Former eBay CEO Meg Whitman is the namesake of one of the university's six residential colleges after donating $30 million. Amazon founder Jeff Bezos has also made significant donations, while the university's largest donation came from oil tycoon William Scheide, who willed the university more than $300 million in rare books.

The country as we know it would not exist if the 1041 system were common knowledge. I'm not suggesting that America would burn to the ground, but we would not have the revenue stream of federal taxation as we know it today. You could also assume that the government would not be spending money it doesn't have, creating massive amounts of debt, or funding frivolous projects. This would also prevent it from laundering newly printed money back to major corporations and donors of the same politicians who write the rules of the game. This systemic division of knowledge is the driving force behind income and wealth disparity.

This is another example how our government has been corrupted since being designed by our Founding Fathers. The United States started without a strong federal government, and the intent of the structure that did exist was only for protection. The tyrannical central bank in England was a major catalyst for the American Revolution, yet there are so many similarities between that system and our current one. Today, the people in power have perfected the game of putting pressure on business owners through taxation, which gives politicians leverage to cut deals that trade tax breaks for donations to their campaigns and personal bank accounts. The wealthy elite understand the game and created a network to pass the information in this book to each other under the guise of philanthropy, which we'll discuss in more detail later in this chapter.

Many of the divisive issues our country has today are due to this flaw. The wealthy elite keep this information secret in order to increase their fortunes and political power. If minority groups knew this information, and were able to take advantage of it to grow their wealth, they would feel a sense of abundance instead of scarcity. They could break free from systemic issues that set them up to fail. People are so much more productive when they feel in control of their lives. Solving this information divide would make huge progress toward leveling the playing field for everyone. Not everyone is a great fit for the 1041 system, and there will always be outliers. However, just having access to the information gives people more choices and freedom, along with the potential of more wealth and production.

I'm not sharing this information to entwine you with a corrupt system, but rather to help you ethically build an economic island where you can escape the corruption. You should not feel guilt, but empowerment, in learning this information. In a dissenting opinion from Commissioner v. Newman, a United States Court of Appeals for the Second Circuit case heard in 1947, Judge Billings Learned Hand wrote "Over and over again courts have said that there is nothing sinister in so arranging one's affairs as to keep taxes as low as possible. Everybody does so, rich or poor; and all do right, for nobody owes any public duty to pay more than the law demands: taxes are enforced exactions, not voluntary contributions. To demand more in the name of morals is a mere cant."

The money the government collects in taxes doesn't even cover the interest expense owed to the Federal Reserve on money we have borrowed. Our tax dollars are so ineffective, and our deficit is so large, that they don't go to pay any of our national debt. Yet, the American dollar is the strongest currency in the world because we're a free society where citizens have the ability to create and produce. Whenever you see governments and central banks working together, colluding in concert, that's when you see societies breaking down due to a thirst for printing more and more money. The end game is what we're currently witnessing: civil unrest. The only way to protect your family is to create an island and disconnect from the chaos.

People tend to follow the herd when it comes to finances and taxes. We do the same thing our parents did, we follow what our friends do, or what our tribe does. More than 99% of all tax related matters in the

United States are handled by the state-licensed accountants and attorneys we discussed in the last chapter. If they are only taught, trained, and educated about the tax code from a state law level, then they won't know about a federally regulated fiduciary trust. Federal law supersedes state law, and the laws governing federal contract trusts fall under the UTC (Universal Trust Code). More than 80 other types of trusts are statutory, or under state guidance. There are real estate investment trusts (REITs), life insurance trusts (LITs), irrevocable trusts, revocable trusts, grantor type trusts, simple trusts, specialized private trusts, etc. Each type is governed by its own set of laws and rules around taxation.

Most accountants and attorneys are only familiar with a few of these types of trusts, and are restricted by the rules of the game that they know. The statutory trust that I hear about most is the grantor type. It's under state jurisdiction, but similar to other statutory trusts, it does not protect assets from the federal government. The veil can be pierced.

Most statutory trusts have specific purposes. Some are asset protection trusts, and others function for estate planning purposes and the transfer of assets. A few types of statutory structures can be beneficial from a tax perspective, however there's only one type of trust that incorporates all three disciplines: tax strategies, asset protection, and estate planning. The specialized private trust is federal, not a statutory type trust, and it is the crown jewel of the 1041 tax system.

A specialized private trust differs from all other trusts, most notably the simple trust, in many ways. The primary difference can be seen in the jurisdiction and fiduciary responsibilities of the trustees. Your state-licensed tax professionals will not know about this. Trust and contract language varies greatly between the 50 states. However, the

UTC is a uniform, federally regulated code, which is why working with an Enrolled Agent or US Tax Court Practitioner is so important.

I did not come across the 1041 trust and foundation system until I was 46 years old. By that time, I had been working, producing, and making money for 20 years. I had been paying taxes that whole time. As my income grew, so did the amount I owed the government. The game I played changed slightly when I became an entrepreneur and minimized the percentage of tax that I owed. I could never keep everything I produced, though. I could never chose to grow and invest in my businesses without the government sticking its grubby hands in the pot. This frustration haunts so many entrepreneurs and business owners. We work so hard to create a legacy and better the world, only to have the government take 50-60% of every dollar we produce! That's not why you go into business, and that's not why our Founding Fathers left tyranny and oppression to create a new country where they made freedom and ownership paramount.

The 1041 system has been buried in plain sight for more than 100 years now. These trusts are ironclad, impenetrable contracts, which people have been using variations of since the 1500s. During the rule of King Henry VIII, as Great Britain extended its empire, knights would return home to see their land and possessions pillaged. The king created a contract whereby the men who fought for him could place their possessions and land in "trust." These assets would be managed and controlled by a designated trustee and returned to their owners upon victory and their return home. That's how these contracts became law. This later became known as British Common Law, or Common Law of Contracts. Any nation governed by Great Britain throughout its expansion fell under this law. It then became the common language for trusts and contracts in most nations, and is the style of language used in the U.S. Constitution, the Bill of Rights, and our legal codes.

Give your tax guru a break

It's critical that you know whose advice to take. To create a legacy that lasts generations, you've got to make sure that the people you follow, and the strategies you implement, are focused on the same target. Most tax professionals have never heard of, or ever filed, a 1041 tax return. It's safe to say that 99.5% of all the clients state-licensed CPAs deal with are in the 1040 world. A lot of federally licensed Enrolled Agents don't even know about the specialized private trust, or how it operates according to the 1041 tax code.

Give your tax professional a break—they don't know this stuff. This is high-level tax strategy and planning typically reserved for politicians, their benefactors, professional athletes, and elite entertainers. According to my research, they usually pay around $500,000 in start-up costs alone, plus hundreds of thousands annually for maintenance at financial institutions, such as Goldman Sachs, UBS, or HSBC. Typically, those institutions will reserve the type of service I'm teaching you about for clients who have a net worth of at least $50 million, and the client must put all accounts with that institution. If you have a net worth under $3 million, a state- licensed tax attorney or CPA might do what you need and reduce your taxes as much as possible. Your savings wouldn't be on par with the 1041 system, but it wouldn't be bad. For those with a net worth of $50 million or higher, maybe HSBC would be a better fit, as they can take care of clients who need more of a full-service attorney and accounting firm. For everyone in between, my firm may be a fit, as we provide a cheaper set up with fewer ongoing costs.

Most tax professionals don't specialize in multiple disciplines. It's been my experience that the 1041 structure requires someone who is an expert in three disciplines: contract law, constitutional law, and tax law. There aren't many CPAs or attorneys who understand contracts written for the specialized private trust structure, let alone how it interacts with the various entities and the private foundation. Rules governing the 1041 specialized private trust are buried deep inside the tax code. Does that sound like something you want your CPA to handle?

The 86 types of statutory trusts all follow a different set of rules and restrictions. One entity is taxed differently than another. For example, the grantor trusts file a 1041 tax return, but an irrevocable life insurance trust does not. If a state-licensed agent doesn't understand this, it's not their fault—blame their training. If someone wants to specialize in corporate law, corporate tax, or become a CFO for a company, then they're going to study the state code that will impact a corporation the most. They are focused on state rules and regulations, not federal contract law, Constitutional law, or tax law that supersedes state law. They only know what they learned in an attempt to pass the state bar or board exam. It's worth repeating that they are not doing a poor job. They didn't do anything wrong. My point is that they don't know what they don't know.

On the 1041 tax return (which you can find on IRS.gov), you'll notice that on the upper left-hand corner of the form, there are nine different entities. That's nine different sets of tax rules, nine sets of guidelines, and nine sets of regulations that your tax guru must understand. The rules of that game can be found in the federal tax code, as well.

In order to know about this stuff, a tax professional would have to be specifically exposed to it. They would either have to have a client who is a 1041 trust and foundation practitioner, be a 1041 practitioner themselves, or be trained by someone in this world. It's not for everyone—it's not for 99.5% of America. I'm not saying the number of families using this system can't grow.

Of course, we can add more members to this elite group. My job is to tell you about the system. Your job is to ask yourself if this applies to you. Do you think this is a good fit for your business, family, and legacy? It's a simple yes or no question, but it is difficult to answer.

Meet the Buffetts and Gates

You are not alone in beginning this journey. You won't be persecuted, condemned, or take an arrow in the back. The 990-PF tax records of some of the 200,000-plus families in the 1041 foundation system are public record and can be viewed at charitynavigator.org. I have studied tax returns from Warren Buffett, Bill Gates, Jeff Bezos, Mark Zuckerberg, and other members of the wealthy elite who have made a life-time commitment to giving away their wealth to charitable causes. They call this commitment The Giving Pledge, and it has been signed by countless billionaires. It was initiated by Buffett as a way to pass wealth-management information on to other elite families. The goal is to generate more wealth, fund philanthropy, and change the world. Find out more about The Giving Pledge and those who are a part of it at www.givingpledge.org. Not too long ago, Bill and Melinda Gates were interviewed on CNBC about the tax-free wealth generated inside the Bill and Melinda Gates Foundation. Melinda immediately acknowledged that the wealth gap is "not fair." She added that she and

Bill will "use whatever influence we have to help as many people as possible, and advance equity around the world."

The 1041 system has worked for entrepreneurs who made a fortune. It has worked for doctors who want to be able to protect themselves from lawsuits, judgments, and creditors. They see the value of the contract clause inside of the trust agreement. This has also worked for farmers who want to transfer land, or the family operations, from generation to generation without incurring probate or estate tax.

Honestly, I always sensed that politicians and celebrities played by a different set of rules.

That's why they are able to grow wealth at an alarming rate. In 1982, the 400 wealthiest Americans had a total wealth of $93 million. Now, it's 25 times that amount. That would not be possible if they had to leak their wealth through taxes. There are several well-known families who have used the 1041 system since the beginning of taxation and are now in the third generation of growing their wealth using uninterrupted compounding.

As you start your journey and uncover the truth about the two different tax systems, you'll start to see how wealth is created in America. Politicians have designed the 1041 system to keep money flowing into their campaigns and use the power of uninterrupted compounding to keep it growing. There is truth behind the expression "the rich get richer, and the poor get poorer." Politics will become a joke to you (if it hasn't already) as you learn how the game is played. Politicians from both sides of the aisle play the same game to manipulate the masses and control the flow of income to keep people reliant on the government for social programs, public works, education, healthcare, and all of the other pleasantries we enjoy today.

The wealthiest families don't play that game, though. They create their own. Warren Buffett grew up understanding the 1041 system. His father, Howard Buffett, learned about the two tax systems while he represented Nebraska in the House of Representatives. Warren Buffett learned from his father as he created business trusts, family trusts, and family foundations. He realized that nothing his family created in terms of wealth was technically "theirs." He grew up in a family who believed they were merely stewards of their blessings. He became passionate about building companies, and started his journey creating Berkshire Hathaway while continuing his family's legacy. Warren's son, Howard G. Buffett, also practices the 1041 system and has his own foundation, The Howard G. Buffett Family Foundation, which receives generous donations from Warren every year. The father-son duo can use their foundations to trade, buy, or sell Berkshire Hathaway stock all tax-free into perpetuity!

Warren Buffett met Bill Gates in 2000, right after Gates and Microsoft had gone through a living hell. The IRS started investigating Microsoft for tax evasion due to income originating in foreign countries. The two billionaires became fast friends. Buffett taught Gates the entire 1041 system and even pledged $34 billion to the newly created Bill and Melinda Gates Foundation, a private 501(c) (3) organization. So what do you think the Gates Foundation did with that donation? The foundation turned around and bought stock in Berkshire Hathaway. Every year, Buffett donates billions to the Gates Foundation in the form of class B shares of Berkshire Hathaway stock (preferred shares of stock, for those who are not familiar). The Gates Foundation has grown to more than $51 billion in value today. How is that possible if they're "giving it all away?" That foundation is one of the largest shareholders of Berkshire Hathaway stock (all tax-free). Now, they're able to buy and sell those assets at will with absolutely no tax. They are able to trade that stock, keep the profits tax-free, and grow that wealth inside the tax-exempt private foundation.

Form 990-PF (2016)				Page **3**
Part IV Capital Gains and Losses for Tax on Investment Income				

	(a) List and describe the kind(s) of property sold (e g , real estate, 2-story brick warehouse, or common stock, 200 shs MLC Co)	(b) How acquired P—Purchase D—Donation	(c) Date acquired (mo , day, yr)	(d) Date sold (mo , day, yr)
1 a	414257 BERKSHIRE HATHAWAY CL B	P	2016-07-13	2016-07-14
b	284266 BERKSHIRE HATHAWAY CL B	P	2016-07-13	2016-07-15
c	114262 BERKSHIRE HATHAWAY CL B	P	2016-07-13	2016-11-16
d	235000 BERKSHIRE HATHAWAY CL B	P	2016-07-13	2016-11-17
e				

	(e) Gross sales price	(f) Depreciation allowed (or allowable)	(g) Cost or other basis plus expense of sale	(h) Gain or (loss) (e) plus (f) minus (g)
a	60,521,007		60,452,524	68,483
b	41,443,885		41,482,937	-39,052
c	17,950,717		16,674,254	1,276,463
d	37,161,232		34,293,550	2,867,682
e				

The Bill and Melinda Gates Foundation does amazing charitable work, but make no mistakes about it, the main reason the Gates use this strategy is to keep and grow wealth. Bill Gates makes no qualms about that fact. He consistently defends tax breaks for foundations, writing that philanthropy is great at "solving tough problems and managing high-risk projects that the government can't take on and corporations won't." Now, imagine that corporations could keep every dollar they make and not pay taxes, but in return they must use the money to give back to the community. I believe that corporations would take on those high-risk projects if that were the case. The Gates Foundation has invested a fortune into the research and development of a malaria vaccine. In 2005, Gates called malaria the "forgotten epidemic," as it was responsible for killing 2,000 African children every day. The initiative was so successful that in 2009, Gates vowed to "develop a new generation of vaccines that are even more effective, and could someday help eradicate malaria altogether." The fight to eradicate malaria continues today, and in 2019 Forbes reported that "After more than thirty years in development and almost $1 billion of investment, a malaria vaccine is now being deployed in three African countries: Malawi, Ghana ... and Kenya, where it is now part of children's routine immunization schedules." The Gates Foundation has also played a major role in developing a COVID-19 vaccine. In 2020, the foundation focused its resources on the global pandemic and pledged $1.75 billion for COVID-19 response and funding underlying vaccine technologies.

The bottom line here is that Gates, and many other philanthropists, would not have been able to come anywhere near this level of generosity without the 1041 trust and foundation system. Hundreds of thousands of other Americans have had success playing this game, too. It works for those who embrace the tax code, can afford a team who know and can follow the law, and want to keep their tax dollars legally and ethically.

efile GRAPHIC print - DO NOT PROCESS	As Filed Data -		DLN: 93491317011197

Form **990-PF**	**Return of Private Foundation**	OMB No 1545-0052
Department of the Treasury Internal Revenue Service	or Section 4947(a)(1) Trust Treated as Private Foundation ▶ **Do not enter social security numbers on this form as it may be made public.** ▶ **Information about Form 990-PF and its instructions is at** _www.irs.gov/form990pf_.	**2016** Open to Public Inspection

For calendar year 2016, or tax year beginning 01-01-2016 , and ending 12-31-2016

Name of foundation BILL & MELINDA GATES FOUNDATION	**A** Employer identification number 56-2618866
Number and street (or P O box number if mail is not delivered to street address) Room/suite PO BOX 23350	**B** Telephone number (see instructions) (206) 709-3100
City or town, state or province, country, and ZIP or foreign postal code SEATTLE, WA 98102	**C** If exemption application is pending, check here ▶ ☐

G Check all that apply ☐ Initial return ☐ Initial return of a former public charity
☐ Final return ☐ Amended return
☐ Address change ☐ Name change

D 1. Foreign organizations, check here ▶ ☐
2. Foreign organizations meeting the 85% test, check here and attach computation ▶ ☐

H Check type of organization ☑ Section 501(c)(3) exempt private foundation
☐ Section 4947(a)(1) nonexempt charitable trust ☐ Other taxable private foundation

E If private foundation status was terminated under section 507(b)(1)(A), check here ▶ ☐

I Fair market value of all assets at end of year *(from Part II, col (c), line 16)*▶$ 41,326,959,325

J Accounting method ☐ Cash ☑ Accrual
☐ Other (specify)
(Part I, column (d) must be on cash basis)

F If the foundation is in a 60-month termination under section 507(b)(1)(B), check here ▶ ☐

Form 990PF Part VIII Line 1 - List all officers, directors, trustees, foundation managers and their compensation

(a) Name and address	Title, and average hours per week (b) devoted to position	(c) Compensation (If not paid, enter -0-)	(d) Contributions to employee benefit plans and deferred compensation	Expense account, (e) other allowances
WILLIAM H GATES III 500 FIFTH AVENUE NORTH SEATTLE, WA 98109	TRUSTEE 25 00	0	0	0
MELINDA FRENCH GATES 500 FIFTH AVENUE NORTH SEATTLE, WA 98109	TRUSTEE 30 00	0	0	0
WARREN E BUFFETT 500 FIFTH AVENUE NORTH SEATTLE, WA 98109	TRUSTEE 1 00	0	0	0
SUSAN DESMOND-HELLMANN 500 FIFTH AVENUE NORTH SEATTLE, WA 98109	CHIEF EXECUTIVE OFFICER 40 00	1,327,312	85,859	0
WILLIAM H GATES SR 500 FIFTH AVENUE NORTH SEATTLE, WA 98109	CO-CHAIR 10 00	0	0	0

"The income tax created more criminals than any other single act of government."

- BarryGoldwater

CHAPTER TEN
CALL TO ACTION

Taxes are, by all definitions, a transfer of ownership (or partial ownership) of your income or assets, a concept known as "split title." We know that taxes follow title, as does liability, for individuals using their social security number when filing a 1040 tax return. State- licensed trust attorneys will likely tell you that the best way to protect your property and investments is to put them into a trust. The problem is that there are more than 86 types of trusts, and many require that you give full responsibility of those assets to a third-party trustee, meaning you will not have control over your investments.

It is extremely important to find out which type of trust you are getting. Each variation must follow different rules of taxation, liability, and fiduciary control (who controls the money and assets). Who the beneficiaries can or cannot be also varies. Each type pertains to a specific part of the tax code. Nine types of trusts file on the 1041 form, which means there are nine sets of rules, regulations, tax deductions, expenditures, and taxable consequences for various types of income. You can find these listed at the top left side of the 1041 tax return.

Now it's time to put this information to work for you. First, find an Enrolled IRS agent. To earn an Enrolled Agent license, tax practitioners must understand all state laws pertaining to tax codes as well as the federal Internal Revenue Code, which is where the magic happens. A great Enrolled Agent looks at the code as a game. They look at the law and ask themselves "how can I apply the law to this scenario and keep more of the tax dollars?" The answers become clear and obvious within the code language itself.

One of the things that my team does on behalf of our clients is get them on a Zoom call with the entire team every quarter. We perform another Gap Map analysis and go over what the client did last quarter, where they are currently, and what they project for the next quarter. This helps everyone stay on the same page, but it also helps us document everything in the different entities. Documentation is key due to the legal concept known as "form over substance." Substance is what the code actually says, but the meaning and intent behind it is the form. You can technically be within the law in substance, but if you're doing it intentionally just to evade taxes, that's not why the system was designed. That's why you have to document everything consistently within the entity: to be able to back up what you're doing in the trust to validate that it's not for your benefit, but for the trust's benefit. That way you're not only following form, but substance, as well.

The biggest problem people run into with these trusts, according to the attorneys on my team, is that they operate according to the law, but not for the right reasons. The form over substance issue is what the IRS specifically targets and goes after. They are looking for people who are trying to follow the rules of the game, but with mal intent. We solve this problem for our clients with the quarterly team meetings. If anyone ever questions what my clients are doing, they have rock-solid documentation to back up everything they did and why they did it.

Using the word "unless" to protect your investments

Have you ever looked at tax code before? The first paragraph of each segment will talk about the topic and the issues that come along with it. Then, the second paragraph lists the rules and how the assets in the particular segment should be taxed. Each section includes a laundry list of things you can or cannot do. It's all the things you would want to do, but are strictly prohibited from doing, unless—now that's an interesting word. In a single word, "unless" can take everything you have said upfront and nullify it.

Imagine you're at a party with the most tempting feast laid on a table in front of you, yet you're at risk for another heart attack and had just gotten your cholesterol levels in check.

Someone hands you a plate. You start salivating, but you can't decide if you should listen to your stomach or your wife's voice in your head. Aromas waft through the air along with sounds of anticipation as a crowd begins grabbing plates and silverware before lining up behind you. You grapple with the consequences of indulging in such a meal: flushing all the work you've done to get back in shape down the drain, the fight you'll have with your spouse if you partake, and the discomfort you'll feel in a few hours. Just as you summon the courage to sidestep out of the line, you utter the word "unless," and now nothing you thought or said before that word matters. You'll only focus on what comes after that word.

That is how we get to do what we want to do without restrictions. If I say "I can't eat that, *unless* I work out hard to burn it off or eat healthy for the next week," you would know I can eat anything I want, as long as I've got a back-up plan. We use "unless" to make exceptions, and the IRS uses it, too.

If you go to IRS.gov and pick out any part of the tax code, you'll see that language throughout. First, it will tell you what you can or cannot do, why it's not a deduction, why it's not considered deductible, or what you must pay in tax for owning something or creating that revenue, *unless...* That's the game-changer. That's the stuff they don't teach the accountants at H&R Block. Skip to the end of the section of tax code and read what it says right after "unless." Sometimes, the government uses the word "except" for the same purpose. Whatever it says after one of these two words is what you are allowed to do—the exception to the law. That's how you can follow the law to keep your tax dollars, grow your wealth, and change your family's lives along with the world around you.

When you're seeking advice from a tax professional, ask them about their knowledge of the tax code. Specifically, the verbiage. Ask how they plan tax strategy for their clients. What sections of the code do they seem to use most? Have they ever sought an Enrolled Agent license, and are they familiar with the specialized private trust and 1041 tax return.

Pre-tax expenditures

Most of the 1041 system lives after "unless." According to tax code found on IRS.gov, pre-tax expenditure is an amount paid or incurred to...

- influence the outcome of any specific public election or carry on any voter registration drive, *unless* certain requirements (explained in influencing elections and carrying on voter registration drives) are satisfied.

- make a grant to an individual for travel, study, or other similar purposes, *unless* certain requirements (explained under grants to individuals) are satisfied.

- make a grant to an organization (other than an organization described in section 509(a)(1), (2), or (3) or an exempt operation foundation) *unless* the foundation exercises expenditure responsibility with the respect to the grant, or...

- carry out any purpose other than a religious, charitable, scientific, literary, or educational purpose, the fostering of national or international amateur sports competition (with exceptions), or the prevention of cruelty to children or animals.

Don't invest like it's the '80s

Much like there is a difference between using an Enrolled Agent or a CPA for your taxes, you've also got to be mindful of the lies Wall Street brokers will tell you. A big one they try to sell is "You've just got to ride out the ups and downs of the market, let the compound interest do its job, and you'll have plenty for retirement." This may have been true back in 1996, when Dave Ramsey, Suze Orman, and company were at the zenith of their "buy term, invest the difference" advice. Quite a bit has changed in the world since those days. In 1996, things were much more local and linear. People were focused on their local economies, and maybe the national economy. The global economy that we know today was in its infancy. Likewise, we could project within a certain degree where markets were going to head. Now, everything is exponential, accelerated by technology and the speed of communication. If you have a great idea and the ability to reach an audience, you can make $1 million practically overnight. You can also go bankrupt much faster because of the debt load you carry and the compounding effect of that debt. Everything compounds—the good and bad. Problems compound, too, unless you interrupt that compounding effect to stop it. Interest will compound, as well, if it's not interrupted.

When Einstein said "The only miracle in mathematics is compound interest," what did he really mean? Was he just using different words to express what all of the talking heads on Wall Street say now? They'll have you believe that if you put money into an account it will average a certain rate of return, compound over time, and you will come out a winner. Unfortunately, that can't be further from the truth, which Einstein clarified upfront. I'd like you to consider the possibility that when you're dealing with returns, the average rate of return does not matter. It has been my experience that most Wall Street brokers use that technique, and so it's probably not what you've been told. It may not be what you want to hear, but it is a fact.

Let's put aside the Wall Street propaganda for a moment. We've heard the Ramsey and Orman mindset since the '80s, which was a time of massive growth in America. Most of the hedge fund managers and financial experts I know have studied market trends since the beginning of their careers. They all agree that America reached its zenith back in the '80s. That decade brought exponential growth in capital markets, as well as real estate and other growth segments. Wealth grew at an alarming rate back then, and the world was very different. We didn't have the internet or mass media as we know them, and social media was nonexistent. You had a handful of local newspapers to choose from, and you could watch three channels: ABC, NBC, and CBS. If you followed real estate trends in your area, you knew what businesses were moving into town and which were shutting down.

Everything seemed local. If Greece had been defaulting half way around the world, we would not have heard much about it. With the exception of the presidential election every four years, we were focused on city, county, and state events. We were focused on our families and our own personal economies a lot more than the global economy. Our family budgets mattered more than the national budget.

Today, everything is global, and information moves around the internet and social media at lightning speed. It's common to hear about economic news, such as Greece defaulting on their currency, or how problems in China may rattle our own markets. Everything is interconnected. It may come as a surprise to you, but Greece has been in financial crisis for more than 90 years.

Greece has only been an independent country since the Treaty of Constantinople in 1831, and they have spent a considerable amount of time struggling with debt. It's been a fact of life over there, but due to the media and internet, we hear all about it now, and it affects our markets.

Wall Street has had such a tight grip on the American public for more than 80 years. As a result, we are at the mercy of the joker brokers and traders, who might as well be at a casino playing with Monopoly money. The stock market is no longer a place to invest your hard-earned income and watch it grow and compound like you've been tricked into believing. In the '80s, the top tax bracket was 70% on income more than $200,000, and the bottom rate was 40%. You could safely defer your taxes and put as much cash into that account as you could, watching it grow while you were productively working. You could have a nest egg to enjoy at retirement, hopefully at a much lower tax rate. It made sense back then. Defer taxes at a higher rate, and spend your money later at a lower rate.

Below is a series of questions I like to ask my clients. As you review them, think about your worldview and the problems you anticipate may arise related to these topics. Try to quantify the cost of not shifting your personal economy to the 1041 system. Consider the purpose of paying taxes to a federal government that is essentially bankrupt. If you don't know an answer, then it's worth your time to do some research and see what you can find.

- Do you think taxes today are lower or higher than the historical average?
- What do you think the average historical tax rate has been?
- Do you think taxes will go up, down, or stay the same in the future?
- You may be shocked to learn that the highest tax rate in history was 94% in 1944-45. What was happening then that would cause the government to aggressively increase taxes?

- Remember, 31 years earlier the government did not collect tax at all. So now do youbelieve taxes will go up, down, or stay the same?

- How will the government pay for unfunded obligations such as Social Security,Medicare, Medicaid, and other programs?

- How will this affect your 401(k), IRA, mutual fund, or retirement account that is tax-deferred?

Your account balance drops when you pull money out to spend at retirement. If the market is as volatile as it is today, and you're withdrawing those funds, how quickly would you run out of money? That's the age-old question Wall Street brokers will never talk about with clients. They don't even want you to ask, but if you want to see them squirm, go ahead.

Constant vs. Fluctuating Returns

Beginning retirement asset value = $1,000,000
Number of years = 30

10% of Beginning Value = ($100,000)
Average return = 14.84%

Constant Returns

Retirement Year	Annual Return	Annual Income	Account Value
1	14.84%	-$100,000	$1,033,290
2	14.84%	-$100,000	$1,072,100
3	14.84%	-$100,000	$1,116,360
4	14.84%	-$100,000	$1,167,188
5	14.84%	-$100,000	$1,225,558
6	14.84%	-$100,000	$1,292,591
7	14.84%	-$100,000	$1,369,572
8	14.84%	-$100,000	$1,457,976
9	14.84%	-$100,000	$1,559,500
10	14.84%	-$100,000	$1,676,090
11	14.84%	-$100,000	$1,809,982
12	14.84%	-$100,000	$1,963,743
13	14.84%	-$100,000	$2,140,322
14	14.84%	-$100,000	$2,343,106
15	14.84%	-$100,000	$2,575,983
20	14.84%	-$100,000	$4,373,434
25	14.84%	-$100,000	$7,963,668
30	14.84%	-$100,000	$15,134,818

Historical Data Source: S&P 500 Total Return Index (w/GFD Extension) (1970-1999); Global Financial Data, Inc., All Rights Reserved. Used with Permission. GFD Extension denotes the extension of data back through time for a data series from its point of origin, potentially even before said index was in existence. Hypothetical illustration may not be used to predict or project investment results. Past performance is no guarantee of future results.

The first returns chart shows you that the best 30 years of the S&P 500 were between 1970 and 2000. The average rate of return during that period was 14.84%. If you retired in 1970 with a nest egg of $1 million and needed to spend $100,000 a year, you would never have to worry about running out of money. Your $1 million would be averaging almost 15% in returns, and you'd only be spending 10%. Make sense?

The second chart breaks down the actual rates of return between the best 30 years of the S&P. It illustrates the problem with the "buy and hold" strategy that Wall Street advisors are fond of pushing.

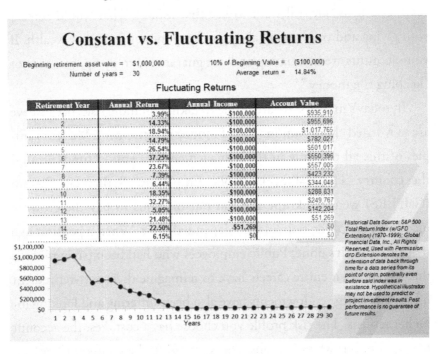

Constant vs. Fluctuating Returns

Beginning retirement asset value = $1,000,000   10% of Beginning Value = ($100,000)
Number of years = 30   Average return = 14.84%

Fluctuating Returns

Retirement Year	Annual Return	Annual Income	Account Value
1	3.99%	-$100,000	$935,910
2	14.33%	-$100,000	$955,696
3	18.94%	-$100,000	$1,017,765
4	-14.79%	-$100,000	$782,027
5	-26.54%	-$100,000	$501,017
6	37.25%	-$100,000	$550,396
7	23.67%	-$100,000	$557,005
8	-7.39%	-$100,000	$423,232
9	6.44%	-$100,000	$344,048
10	18.35%	-$100,000	$268,831
11	32.27%	-$100,000	$249,767
12	-5.05%	-$100,000	$142,204
13	21.48%	-$100,000	$51,269
14	22.50%	-$51,269	$0
15	6.15%	$0	$0

Historical Data Source: S&P 500 Total Return Index (w/GFD Extension) (1970-1999), Global Financial Data, Inc., All Rights Reserved, Used with Permission. GFD Extension denotes the extension of data back through time for a data series from its point of origin, potentially even before said index was in existence. Hypothetical illustration may not be used to predict or project investment results. Past performance is no guarantee of future results.

When you understand the true nature of compounding, and real vs. theoretical returns, then you will realize that how much it is interrupted matters. This little detail can be the difference between choosing what accounts to stash your cash in, and what accounts to avoid. When looking at "averages." throughout history, your broker is only theorizing and playing games with you. Market volatility and uncertainty make this choice more important than ever before. If you're trying to build wealth consistently so that you can use it to invest, grow, and give, then you can't afford to play it in the Wall Street Casino. You're putting your entire family legacy at risk if you keep your long-term savings in a volatile account. The third chart shows fluctuating returns. If you had that $1 million nest egg in a volatile account between 1970 and 2000, and spent $100,000 each year, you would run out of money in 14 years! This chart shows a drastic drop in value when you see fluctuating returns but still want to use that money. That would impact your giving and your overall ability to keep money and grow wealth. If your accounts are fluctuating and not guaranteed to go up, you are not "keeping the money."

In today's markets, we are prone to taking on more risks because we are so worried about running out of money in retirement. We see examples of this all the time in the management of pension funds around the country. The California Public Employees' Retirement System (CalPERS) went bankrupt and ran out of funds to pay the growing income needs of the retirees who depended on it. When a pension like that runs out, it's done. Public employees who had been paying into it throughout their entire careers have to reimagine their post-retirement lifestyles. College endowments have also been suffering and looking for higher returns. The risk profile you choose has a cost. Yes, the account may go up, but when it drops, you're resetting the compounding and losing money. Wall Street pushes the illusion that "compound interest" is actually happening in our 401(k) and IRA accounts, but when the compounding is interrupted, it stops and has to start all over again at a lower valuation.

Learn how to *give it all away.*

Fundamentally, our system of government is based on principles of human behavior. There are fundamental truths about us that are unavoidable because they are part of our DNA makeup, such as our lizard brains. To review, when I say lizard brain, I'm referring to our limbic system, which is responsible for the fight or flight response that prepares us for anything that may be attacking.

When I was a child, I remember my mother inviting her friends and their children over to our house. Every time they came over, I would run up to my room, gather every toy I could fit in my arms, and yell *"mine, mine, mine!"* My mother thought this was as cute as it was ridiculous, and she never let me forget about it. My lizard brain was on fire whenever I felt like someone might take my things. This is a fundamental knee-jerk reaction that we all have when we feel threatened. Unfortunately, that reaction only strengthens as we get older. We believe everything we have is "ours" because we "earned" it.

The fact is that everything around us is simply a gift that has been given to us for the short time we're here on earth. When we pass away, it is passed on to someone else. Nothing we have today will last, except your legacy and the impact you make on others. Due to human nature, we tend to believe that we have created our lives. Sure, we decide how we spend our days, and control our patterns and habits to some extent. However, as hard as you work, and as much value as you bring to the table to create the world around you, you did not do this alone.

You didn't create that company or come up with that invention by yourself. Your gifts and passions were given to you by someone else at birth. You were predestined with the pieces and parts that make you great.

It's incumbent upon all of us to realize that we are only stewards of our gifts. It's up to us to protect what we've been given, cherish each gift, and multiply them to help others. God helps others through you, so it's your job to create a life where you are the steward of what you've been entrusted with and respect that responsibility. The best way to pull that off is to focus on your purpose, which will energize you and give you guidance when you feel lost. It will be your touch stone, your true north. When you begin to live with purpose and meaning, the whole world will open up to you. You will be connected at the right time with the right people, who have the resources to pull off what used to seem impossible.

A problem we have as humans is that we don't learn from the past. We continuously hit our heads against the wall and make the same mistakes over and over. This disconnects us from God and our purpose. If you believe, as I do, that God is love, then relax in His love and let God connect you to what you need to fulfill that purpose. It's almost magical. Things happen fast when you align yourself with God and His purpose for you.

The magic happens when we make ourselves aware of God's presence. The more we become intentional about spending time with God and listening to His voice, the more aligned our actions become with our purpose. This also make us more secure in who we are and makes us realize that nothing can separate us from Him or our purpose. When we align our actions and purpose, we can focus on going to war for love and unity. When you wake up passionate and on fire each day, that's when life becomes beautiful!

I strongly believe that if you are being a good steward of what you've been blessed with, you will truly understand the meaning and purpose behind the principle that you don't own anything. The 1041 trust and foundation system forces you to act this way. It forces you to give up ownership of your stuff and focus on stewardship. Your foundation will allow you to live a life of purpose and meaning. It will allow you to focus on your personal economy, stop the bleeding, and stop squandering the blessings God has given you. It forces you to manage your resources and assets, grow wealth, and live by the principles in the Parable of the Three Tenants: don't bury or squander your treasure, but multiply it. When you do that, everything changes.

While you give up ownership in the 1041 system, you never lose control of the assets you put in trusts or foundations. This is the principle that built generational wealth for families like the Rockefellers, Vanderbilts, Kennedys, and Mellons. I want to return to Nelson's Rockefeller's quote from Chapter Nine: "The secret to success is to own nothing, but control everything." This reveals how the mindset of the wealthiest families in America differs from the rest of the country. Families with this much wealth focus on contribution, rather than ownership, as soon as they learn about the 1041 system. The same can be true for you. Once you see the structure and behavior of the trust and foundation system, you will understand why giving up ownership, while maintaining control, must be the main goal.

If you are still reading, then chances are you think you may be in the small minority of Americans who are a good fit for the 1041 system. The next logical step is one of self-discovery. If you haven't already, start asking your tax people some questions. I implore you to do your own research. Then, visit www.TheTruthAboutTaxes.org, where you will find a documentary with more information about the specialized private trust and foundation system in this book.

My goal is to work with people who will be committed to this journey, not just interested.

In Matthew 7:6, Jesus explains: "Don't waste what is holy on people who are unholy. Don't throw your pearls to pigs! They will trample the pearls and turn against you." If you more than appreciate the value in this lifestyle, and you're ready to commit to changing your wealth strategy and legacy, I'll be ready to help.

BIBLIOGRAPHY

"2020 KIDS COUNT Data Book Interactive." *The Annie E. Casey Foundation*, www.aecf.org/ interactive/databook/.

"Andrew Jackson Shuts down Second Bank of the U.S." *History. com*, A&E Television Networks, 16 Nov. 2009, www.history. com/this-day-in-history/andrew-jackson-shuts-down-second-bank-of-the-u-s.

Arrillaga-Andreessen, Laura. *Giving 2.0: Transform Your Giving and Our World*. Jossey-Bass, 2012.

Attwood, Janet Bray, and Chris Attwood. *The Passion Test: the Effortless Path to Discovering Your Destiny*. Pocket, 2009.

Barham, James A. "The 100 Richest Universities: Their Generosity and Commitment to Research." *TheBestSchools.org*, Thebestschools.org, 13 Sept. 2019, thebestschools.org/ features/ richest-universities-endowments-generosity-research/.

"Biggest Needs in Texas Foster Care and Adoption ·Foster Care and Adoption · Buckner International." *Buckner International*, 1 Jan. 1970, www.buckner.org/ fostercareadoptionneeds/.

"Bill Gates Announces $168 Million to Develop Next-Generation Malaria Vaccine." *The Bill & Melinda Gates Foundation*, The Bill & Melinda Gates Foundation, 1 Sept. 2008, www. gatesfoundation.org/Media-Center/Press-Releases/2008/09/

Bill-Gates-Announces-168-Million-to-Develop-NextGeneration-Malaria- Vaccine#:~:text=NEW%20YORK%20%2D%2D%20Bill%20Gates,of%20African%20chil dren%20every%20day.

"Foster Care Statistics." *Pathways Youth & Family Services*, www.pathway.org/programs/foster- care/statistics/.

"Gates Foundation Commits $258.3 Million for Malaria Research and Development." *The Bill & Melinda Gates Foundation*, The Bill & Melinda Gates Foundation, 1 Jan. 2005, www.gatesfoundation.org/Media-Center/Press-Releases/2005/10/Gates-Foundation- Commits-2583-Million-for-Malaria-Research.

Harris, Caroline L. "The President vs. A 'Learned Hand.'" *U.S. Chamber of Commerce*, 5 Aug. 2015, www.uschamber.com/above-the-fold/the-president-vs-learned- hand#:~:text=Over%20and%20over%20again%20courts,enforced%20exactions%2C%20n ot%20voluntary%20contributions. 2015, www.uschamber.com/above-the-fold/the-president-vs-learned-hand.

"History." *Frances C. Arrillaga Alumni Center*, alumnicenter.alumni.stanford.edu/history.

Keynes, John Maynard. *The General Theory of Employment, Interest, and Money ; and, Essays in Persuasion*. Classic Books America, 2009.

Mejia, Zameena. "In Their 2018 Annual Letter, Bill and Melinda Gates Share the Secret to Their Optimism." *CNBC*, CNBC, 13 Feb. 2018, www.cnbc.com/2018/02/13/bill-and-melinda-gates-share-secret-to-optimism-in-2018-annual-letter.html?&qsearchterm=melinda+gates.

"Reactive Attachment Disorder." *Mayo Clinic*, Mayo Foundation for Medical Education and Research, 13 July 2017, www.

mayoclinic.org/diseases-conditions/reactive-attachment- disorder/ symptoms-causes/syc-20352939.

Richardson, Gary, and Jessie Romero. "The Meeting at Jekyll Island." *Federal Reserve History*, 4 Dec. 2015, www.federalreservehistory. org/essays/jekyll-island-conference.

Somauroo, Dr. James. "Malaria Vaccine 30 Years And $1 Billion In The Making Now Deployed In Third Country." *Forbes*, Forbes Magazine, 25 Sept. 2019, www.forbes.com/sites/ jamessomauroo/2019/09/24/malaria-vaccine-30-years-and- 1-billion-in-the-making-now- deployed-in-third-country/?sh= 3b423cc52583.

Taylor, Kenneth Nathaniel. *The Living Bible, Paraphrased*. Tyndale House, 1983. Translation, Bible English New Living. *Holy Bible, New Living Translation*. Tyndale House Publishers, 1996.

Weise, Elizabeth. "Bill Gates Warned about a Pandemic; and Enough about Microchips, He Says." *USA Today*, Gannett Satellite Information Network, 27 Jan. 2021, www.usatoday.com/story/ news/health/2021/01/27/bill-gates-annual-letter-pandemic- planning-vaccines-microchips/6700910002/.

Made in the USA
Middletown, DE
04 November 2024

63884743R00086